M. M. (Milton M.) Shaw

**9000 Miles on a Pullman Train**

M. M. (Milton M.) Shaw

**9000 Miles on a Pullman Train**

ISBN/EAN: 9783744723640

Printed in Europe, USA, Canada, Australia, Japan

Cover: Foto ©Andreas Hilbeck / pixelio.de

More available books at **www.hansebooks.com**

# Nine Thousand Miles

# On A Pullman Train

AN ACCOUNT

OF A

## Tour of Railroad Conductors

FROM PHILADELPHIA

TO THE

PACIFIC COAST AND RETURN

BY M. M. SHAW

PHILADELPHIA
ALLEN, LANE & SCOTT, PRINTERS AND PUBLISHERS
Nos. 1211-13 Clover Street
1898

Entered, according to Act of Congress, in the year 1898,
BY M. M. SHAW,
In the office of the Librarian of Congress, at Washington.

TO THE TRUE AND LOYAL WOMEN

OF OUR PARTY,

THE BELOVED AND CHERISHED COMPANIONS

OF OUR HEARTHS AND HOMES,

THIS BOOK IS AFFECTIONATELY DEDICATED.

# INDEX TO ILLUSTRATIONS.

| | | |
|---|---|---|
| M. M. Shaw | . . . . . Frontispiece. | |
| George W. Boyd, Assistant General Passenger Agent, Pennsylvania Railroad | Face page | 6 |
| Broad Street Station, Philadelphia | " | 12 |
| A Pullman Dining Car | " | 16 |
| C. E. Wyman, Chairman of the Committee | " | 18 |
| A Pullman Sleeping Car | " | 22 |
| Sang Hollow on the Conemaugh, Pennsylvania Railroad, | " | 28 |
| At Effingham, Illinois | " | 34 |
| Leaving Longview Junction, Texas | " | 34 |
| At Fort Worth, Texas | " | 36 |
| O. H. Bacon, Conductor Texas and Pacific Railway | " | 38 |
| A Group at Van Horn, Texas | " | 40 |
| Tom McDonald and Fred Beach | " | 40 |
| Myrtle Taylor on a Bronco | " | 42 |
| Residence of Jacob Hand, Sierra Blanca, Texas | " | 42 |
| Flooded District, Alfalfa, Texas | " | 52 |
| Wrecked by Train Robbers on Southern Pacific Railway, | " | 52 |
| William J. Maxwell, of the Committee | " | 56 |
| Col. Si Ryan | " | 60 |
| Arizona Landscape | " | 66 |
| "Yuma Bill," Indian Chief at Yuma, over 100 years old, | " | 66 |
| The California Poppy | " | 68 |
| A Cluster of Navel Oranges, California | " | 72 |
| Winter in Southern California | " | 74 |
| Brookside Avenue, Redlands, California | " | 76 |
| San Gabriel Mission, California | " | 78 |
| Giant Palms on the road to San Gabriel | " | 78 |
| An Avenue in Pasadena, California | " | 80 |
| Great Cable Incline, Mt. Lowe Railway | " | 82 |
| Echo Mountain House and Car on the 48 Per Cent. Grade, Mt. Lowe Railway | " | 84 |
| Mt. Lowe Railway, California | " | 86 |
| Circular Bridge, Mt. Lowe Railway, California | " | 88 |
| Ye Alpine Tavern, Mt. Lowe, California | " | 90 |
| T. S. C. Lowe | " | 92 |
| George W. Brown, of the Committee | " | 98 |
| New Cliff House and Seal Rocks, San Francisco, Cal. | " | 102 |
| Parapet, Sutro Heights, San Francisco, Cal. | " | 104 |

## INDEX TO ILLUSTRATIONS.

| | |
|---|---|
| John H. Reagan, of the Committee | Face page 112 |
| Hercules' Pillars, Columbia River, Oregon | " 120 |
| The Columbia River | " 124 |
| J. P. O'Brien, Superintendent Rail Lines, Oregon Railroad and Navigation Company | " 126 |
| Mt. Adams, Washington | " 128 |
| Mt. St. Helens, from Portland, Oregon | " 128 |
| Multnomah Falls, Oregon | " 130 |
| Along the Columbia River | " 132 |
| C Street, Tacoma, Washington | " 134 |
| Bridge, Point Defiance Park, Tacoma, Washington | " 134 |
| Latourelle Falls, Oregon | " 136 |
| The Hobo Passenger | " 138 |
| Crossing Columbia River on the "Tacoma" | " 138 |
| Elevator A, Tacoma, Washington | " 140 |
| Shore of Lake Pend d'Oreille at Hope, Idaho | " 140 |
| Spokane Falls, Spokane, Washington | " 142 |
| Spokane, Washington | " 142 |
| W. B. Hale, Conductor Northern Pacific Railway | " 144 |
| "Dan," Salt Lake City Railroad Station, Utah | " 154 |
| Grave of Brigham Young, Salt Lake City, Utah | " 154 |
| The Mormon Temple and Square, Salt Lake City, Utah | " 160 |
| Chas. E. Hooper, of the Denver and Rio Grande Railroad | " 166 |
| Bathing Pool at Glenwood Springs, Colorado | " 168 |
| In the Pool at Glenwood Springs | " 168 |
| Walter W. Terry, of the Committee | " 174 |
| Colonel and Mrs. Mitchell at Marshall Pass | " 178 |
| The "Committee" at Marshall Pass | " 178 |
| The Royal Gorge and the Hanging Bridge, Grand Cañon of the Arkansas | " 182 |
| Ascent of Pike's Peak by Manitou and Pike's Peak Railroad (cog wheel) | " 184 |
| Gateway to the Garden of the Gods, Colorado; Pike's Peak in the Distance | " 186 |
| On Pike's Peak—Altitude, 14,147 feet | " 188 |
| Bride and Groom at Balance Rock, Garden of the Gods, Colorado | " 190 |
| Manitou Springs, Colorado | " 192 |
| Bachelors and Burros in the Garden of the Gods | " 196 |
| "Who are we? Who are we? P. P. C.! Cooks, Waiters, and Porters of the O. R. C.!" | " 202 |
| The "232." McCook, Nebraska | " 202 |

# INTRODUCTION.

THE writer is not sure that this work will give satisfation to his many friends who have asked for it; the experience of one is not the experience of all, and many incidents will be remembered, undoubtedly, by different members of the party that are not mentioned in these pages, from the fact that they are unknown to the narrator, not having come under his observation. The difficulty lies in producing an account of our trip from personal notes that will meet the expectation of all. The chief object of this book is to furnish interesting information relative to the party's whereabouts from day to day, giving the names of many kind friends who did so much toward making our journey an interesting and happy one, and who will ever be remembered with feelings of the highest regard by each member of the party. The writer has no apology to offer to critics. Geographical inaccuracies and grammatical inconsistencies can either be accepted or overlooked, at the pleasure of the reader, whom the author hopes will be charitable enough to believe that he believes what he has written, whether it is true or not.

Shortly after the meeting of the twenty-fifth session of the Grand Division of the Order of Railway Conductors at Atlanta, Ga., in May, 1895, a few of the Pennsylvania Railroad conductors running into Broad Street Station, Philadelphia, got together and started a movement toward the organization of a party to visit the twenty-sixth session, in Los Angeles, Cal., in May, 1897. Mr. Chas. E. Wyman was chosen president and manager and Mr. Wm. J. Maxwell secretary and treasurer of the club. It was known as the *Pennsylvania Railroad Conductors' Excursion*. Meetings were held from time to time to complete the organization, formulate plans, and perfect arrangements, and George H. Holgate, Esq., president of the Association of American Inventors, kindly gave the use of his large, comfortable office in the Betz Building, on Broad Street, Philadelphia, for this purpose. A friend of Manager Wyman designed an unique and handsome card, which was submitted to Stephen Greene, Esq., who lithographed and printed several thousand and generously presented them to the excursion. The committee called at the clothing establishment of Wanamaker & Brown, Sixth and Market Streets, to purchase tourist caps for use of the party on the trip, and were liberally provided with all they wanted, free of cost, by the kind and generous members of the firm. The officials of the Pennsylvania Railroad looked with favor upon the scheme, and it was largely due to their kindly efforts and influence that the excursion was such a grand success.

Mr. George W. Boyd, Assistant General Passenger Agent, interested himself greatly in our trip, and under his direction the Tourist Department outlined and arranged the itinerary, which was printed in neat form and presented to the party by Allen, Lane & Scott. This itinerary is published in these pages in its original form, and while the route was adhered to it will be noticed we ran about three days late, delayed by a washout east of El Paso.

Many of the illustrations in this book were prepared from photographs taken by members of the party, also from photographs kindly presented to the author by Prof. T. S. C. Lowe. We are also indebted to the Oregon Railroad and Navigation Company, Northern Pacific Railway Company, and Denver and Rio Grande Railroad Company for illustrations of scenery along their lines.

Our treatment by officers of the Pullman Company was extremely satisfactory, their generosity being highly appreciated. To one and all of these gentlemen who so kindly contributed toward our happiness and pleasure the Pennsylvania Railroad Conductors' Excursion gives, through the writer, a rousing vote of thanks.

M. M. S.

GEO. W. BOYD, ASSISTANT GENERAL PASSENGER AGENT,
PENNSYLVANIA RAILROAD COMPANY.

DETAILED TIME-TABLE AND CONDENSED

# ITINERARY

OF THE

## PENNSYLVANIA RAILROAD CONDUCTORS' TOUR TO THE GOLDEN GATE.

|Miles from Philad'a.| | | |
|---|---|---|---|

SATURDAY, MAY 8, 1897.
Via Pennsylvania Railroad.
    Lv. Philadelphia, Pa. . . . . . (*Eastern time*) 10.30 A. M.
354  Ar. Pittsburgh, Pa. . . . . . .   "   8.15 P. M.
   "  Pittsburgh, Pa. . . . . . . (*Central time*) 7.15 "
             Via Pennsylvania Lines.
    Lv. Pittsburgh, Pa. . . . . . .   "   7.30 "

SUNDAY, MAY 9, 1897.
Via Pennsylvania Lines.
728  Ar. Indianapolis, Ind. . . . . . (*Central time*) 7.00 A. M.
             Via Vandalia Line.
    Lv. Indianapolis, Ind. . . . . .   "   7.10 "
968  Ar. St. Louis, Mo. . . . . . .   "   1.40 P. M.
          Via St. Louis, Iron Mountain & Southern Railway.
    Lv. St. Louis, Mo. . . . . . . (*Central time*) 8.15 "

MONDAY, MAY 10, 1897.
Via St. Louis, Iron Mountain & Southern Railway.
1313  Ar. Little Rock, Ark. . . . . . (*Central time*) 7.10 A. M.
1458  "  Texarkana, Tex. . . . . .   "   12.35 P. M.
             Via Texas & Pacific Railway.
    Lv. Texarkana, Tex. . . . . .   "   1.05 "
1711  Ar. Fort Worth, Tex. . . . . .   "   9.24 "

TUESDAY, MAY 11, 1897.
Via Texas & Pacific Railway.
2326  Ar. El Paso, Tex . . . . . . . (*Central time*) 9.25 "
    (At El Paso Central time changes to Pacific time,
             two hours slower.)

|Miles from Philad'a.| | |

### WEDNESDAY, MAY 12, 1897.
#### Via Southern Pacific Company.

|       | Lv. El Paso, Tex . . . . . . . (*Pacific time*) | 8.00 A. M. |
|-------|---|---|
| 2414  | Ar. Deming, N. M. . . . . . .      "           | 11.00 " |
| 2638  | "  Tucson, N. M. . . . . . .       "           | 7.00 P. M. |

### THURSDAY, MAY 13, 1897.
#### · Via Southern Pacific Company.

| 3008 | Ar. Indio, Cal. . . . . . . . . (*Pacific time*) | 7.00 A. M. |
|------|---|---|
| 3138 | "  Los Angeles, Cal. . . . . .     "            | 12.00 NOON. |

Train to be sidetracked for occupancy.

### MONDAY, MAY 17, 1897.
#### Via Southern Pacific Company.

| 3138 | Lv. Los Angeles, Cal. . . . . . (*Pacific time*) | 2.00 P. M. |

### TUESDAY, MAY 18, 1897.
#### Via Southern Pacific Company.

| 3585 | Ar. San Francisco, Cal. . . . . (*Pacific time*) | 10.00 A. M. |

### THURSDAY, MAY 20, 1897.
#### Via Southern Pacific Company.

| | Lv. San Francisco, Cal. . . . . (*Pacific time*) | 7.00 P. M. |

### SATURDAY, MAY 22, 1897.
#### Via Southern Pacific Company.

| 4357 | Ar. Portland, Ore. . . . . . . (*Pacific time*) | 7.00 A. M. |

Train to be sidetracked for occupancy.

### SUNDAY, MAY 23, 1897.
#### Via Northern Pacific Railway.

|      | Lv. Portland, Ore. . . . . . . (*Pacific time*) | 8.45 A. M. |
|------|---|---|
| 4501 | Ar. Tacoma, Wash. . . . . . .      "            | 2.00 P. M. |

Train to be sidetracked for occupancy.

| | Lv. Tacoma, Wash. . . . . . .      "            | 10.30 " |

(At Hope Pacific time changes to Mountain time, one hour faster.)
Stop at Spokane two hours.

### TUESDAY, MAY 25, 1897.
#### Via Northern Pacific Railway.

| 5283 | Ar. Helena, Mont. . . . . . . (*Mountain time*) | 7.00 A. M. |

Via Great Northern Railway.

## ON A PULLMAN TRAIN.

Miles from Philad'a.

|  | | |
|---|---|---|
| Lv. Helena, Mont. . . . . . . (*Mountain time*) | 12.00 NOON. |
| 5355 Ar. Butte, Mont. . . . . . .   " | 3.00 P. M. |

Train to be sidetracked for occupancy.
Via Montana Union Railway.

|  | | |
|---|---|---|
| Lv. Butte, Mont. . . . . . .   " | 10.00 " |
| 5362 Ar. Silver Bow, Mont. . . . .   " | 10.20 " |

Via Oregon Short Line Railroad.

Lv. Silver Bow, Mont. . . . . (*Mountain time*) 10.30 "

### WEDNESDAY, MAY 26, 1897.

Via Ogden Short Line Railroad.

5752 Ar. Ogden, Utah . . . . . . (*Mountain time*) 11.00 A. M.

Via Rio Grande Western Railway.

|  | | |
|---|---|---|
| Lv. Ogden, Utah . . . . . . (*Mountain time*) | 11.00 " |
| 5789 Ar. Salt Lake City, Utah . .   " | 12.00 NOON. |

Train to be sidetracked for occupancy.

### THURSDAY, MAY 27, 1897.

Via Rio Grande Western Railway.

Lv. Salt Lake City, Utah . . (*Mountain time*) 9.00 P. M.

### FRIDAY, MAY 28, 1897.

6080 Ar. Grand Junction, Col. . . (*Mountain time*) 8.30 A. M.

Via Denver & Rio Grande Railroad.

|  | | |
|---|---|---|
| Lv. Grand Junction, Col. . . (*Mountain time*) | 9.00 " |
| 6169 Ar. Glenwood Springs, Col. .   " | 12.00 NOON. |
| Lv. Glenwood Springs, Col. .   " | 2.00 P. M. |
| Ar. Minturn, Col. . . . . . .   " | 4.10 " |
| " Leadville, Col. . . . . .   " | 6.00 " |
| Lv. Leadville, Col. . . . . .   " | 6.40 " |
| 6319 Ar. Salida, Col. . . . . . . .   " | 8.30 " |

### SATURDAY, MAY 29, 1897.

Via Denver & Rio Grande Railroad.
By D. & R. G. special train.

|  | | |
|---|---|---|
| Lv. Salida, Col. . . . . . . . (*Mountain time*) | 8.00 A. M. |
| Ar. Marshall Pass, Col. . . .   " | 9.40 " |
| Lv. Marshall Pass, Col. . . .   " | 10.20 " |
| 6369 Ar. Salida, Col. . . . . . .   " | 12.00 NOON. |
| Lv. Salida, Col. . . . . . . .   " | 1.00 P. M. |
| Ar. Royal Gorge, Col. . . . .   " | 2.45 " |
| 6511 " Colorado Springs, Col. .   " | 6.00 " |

Train to be sidetracked for occupancy.

10 NINE THOUSAND MILES

Miles
from
Philad'a.

### SUNDAY, MAY 30, 1897.
At Colorado Springs and Manitou.

### MONDAY, MAY 31, 1897.
Via Denver & Rio Grande Railroad.

      Lv. Colorado Springs, Col. . (*Mountain time*) 2.00 A. M.
6586  Ar. Denver, Col. . . . . . .      "      6.00 "
      Train to be sidetracked for occupancy.

### TUESDAY, JUNE 1, 1897.

### WEDNESDAY, JUNE 2, 1897.
At Denver.

### THURSDAY, JUNE 3, 1897.
Via Burlington Route.

      Lv. Denver, Col. . . . . . . (*Mountain time*) 12.01 A. M.
      (At McCook, Neb., Mountain time changes to Central time, one hour faster.)
      Ar. Lincoln, Neb. . . . . . . . (*Central time*) 3.05 "
7124  " Omaha, Neb. . . . . . . .    "    5.00 P. M.
      Lv. Omaha, Neb. . . . . . . .    "    6.30 "

### FRIDAY, JUNE 4, 1897.
Via Burlington Route.

7632  Ar. Chicago, Ill. . . . . . . . (*Central time*) 9.15 A. M.
      Via Pennsylvania Lines.
      Lv. Chicago, Ill. . . . . . . .    "    5.40 P. M.

### SATURDAY, JUNE 5, 1897.
Via Pennsylvania Lines.

8100  Ar. Pittsburg, Pa. . . . . . . . (*Central time*) 6.10 A. M.
      " Pittsburg, Pa. . . . . . . . (*Eastern time*) 7.10 "
      Via Pennsylvania Railroad.
      Lv. Pittsburg, Pa. . . . . . . .    "    7.15 "
8454  " Philadelphia, Pa. . . . . .    "    4.20 P. M.

## LIST OF PASSENGERS.

Mr. G. W. Brown . . . . . . . . . . . . Philadelphia, Pa.
Mrs. G. W. Brown . . . . . . . . . . . .     "
Mr. P. J. Barrett . . . . . . . . . . . Bristol, Pa.
Miss Anna S. Barrett . . . . . . . . .     "
Mr. J. N. Climenson . . . . . . . . . . Philadelphia, Pa.
Mrs. J. N. Climenson . . . . . . . . .     "
Mr. I. M. Cohee . . . . . . . . . . . .     "
Mrs. I. M. Cohee . . . . . . . . . . .     "
Mr. J. B. Crispen . . . . . . . . . . . Renovo, Pa.
Mr. James Dougherty . . . . . . . . . . Trenton, N. J.
Mrs. J. Dougherty . . . . . . . . . . .     "
Mr. T. J. Denniston . . . . . . . . . . Jersey City, N. J.
Mr. G. W. Dale . . . . . . . . . . . . Philadelphia, Pa.
Mrs. G. W. Dale . . . . . . . . . . . .     "
Mr. R. T. Elder . . . . . . . . . . . .     "
Mrs. R. T. Elder . . . . . . . . . . .     "
Mr. R. J. Foulon . . . . . . . . . . .     "
Mrs. R. J. Foulon . . . . . . . . . . .     "
Mr. C. E. Foster . . . . . . . . . . .     "
Mrs. C. E. Foster . . . . . . . . . . .     "
Mr. J. W. Goff . . . . . . . . . . . . Camden, N. J.
Mrs. J. W. Goff . . . . . . . . . . . .     "
Mr. T. B. Gilliland . . . . . . . . . . Harrisburg, Pa.
Mrs. T. B. Gilliland . . . . . . . . .     "
Mr. M. M. Houston . . . . . . . . . . . Norristown, Pa.
Mrs. M. M. Houston . . . . . . . . . .     "
Mr. W. A. Haas . . . . . . . . . . . . Allegheny City, Pa.
Mr. H. R. Haefner . . . . . . . . . . . Columbia, Pa.
Mrs. H. R. Haefner . . . . . . . . . .     "
Mr. S. W. Horner . . . . . . . . . . . Philadelphia, Pa.
Mrs. S. W. Horner . . . . . . . . . . .     "
Mr. S. N. Kilgore . . . . . . . . . . .     "
Mrs. S. N. Kilgore . . . . . . . . . .     "
Mr. T. J. McKernan . . . . . . . . . . Jersey City, N. J.
Mrs. T. J. McKernan . . . . . . . . . .     "
Mr. E. A. Kalkman . . . . . . . . . . . Baltimore, Md.
Mrs. E. A. Kalkman . . . . . . . . . .     "
Mr. Hugh Leary . . . . . . . . . . . . Norristown, Pa.
Mrs. Hugh Leary . . . . . . . . . . . .     "
Mr. J. T. Layfield . . . . . . . . . . Wilmington, Del.
Mrs. J. T. Layfield . . . . . . . . . .     "
Mr. J. M. Matthews . . . . . . . . . . Norristown, Pa.
Mrs. J. M. Matthews . . . . . . . . . .     "

Mr. W. J. Maxwell . . . . . . . . . . . Philadelphia, Pa.
Mrs. W. J. Maxwell . . . . . . . . . . "
Mr. J. H. Moore . . . . . . . . . . . . Manasquan, N. J.
Mrs. J. H. Moore . . . . . . . . . . . "
Mr. C. J. McCarty . . . . . . . . . . Columbia, Pa.
Mr. C. R. Mattson, M. D. . . . . . . . Philadelphia, Pa.
Mrs. C. R. Mattson . . . . . . . . . . "
Mr. W. H. Morris . . . . . . . . . . Wilmington, Del.
Mrs. W. H. Morris . . . . . . . . . . "
Mr. Roland Mitchell . . . . . . . . . Baltimore, Md.
Mrs. Roland Mitchell . . . . . . . . "
Mr. W. H. Post . . . . . . . . . . . . Philadelphia, Pa.
Miss Ella L. Post . . . . . . . . . . . "
Mr. J. A. Reilly . . . . . . . . . . . . "
Mrs. J. A. Reilly . . . . . . . . . . . "
Mr. J. H. Reagan . . . . . . . . . . . "
Mr. J. J. Restein . . . . . . . . . . . Delmar, Del.
Mr. C. L. Springer . . . . . . . . . . Philadelphia, Pa.
Mrs. C. L. Springer . . . . . . . . . "
Mr. L. E. Sheppard . . . . . . . . . . Camden, N. J.
Mrs. L. E. Sheppard . . . . . . . . . "
Mr. M. M. Shaw . . . . . . . . . . . . West Chester, Pa.
Mrs. M. M. Shaw . . . . . . . . . . . "
Mr. C. H. Sloane . . . . . . . . . . . Philadelphia, Pa.
Mr. J. G. Schuler . . . . . . . . . . . Pittsburgh, Pa.
Mr. C. F. Smith . . . . . . . . . . . York, Pa.
Mrs. C. F. Smith . . . . . . . . . . . "
Mr. D. R. Sparks . . . . . . . . . . . Camden, N. J.
Mrs. D. R. Sparks . . . . . . . . . . "
Mr. W. W. Terry . . . . . . . . . . . Philadelphia, Pa.
Mrs. W. W. Terry . . . . . . . . . . . "
Mr. H. H. Taylor . . . . . . . . . . . Trenton, N. J.
Mr. C. E. Waddington . . . . . . . . Philadelphia, Pa.
Mr. Oscar Williams . . . . . . . . . "
Mr. C. E. Wyman . . . . . . . . . . . Moores, Pa.
Mrs. C. E. Wyman . . . . . . . . . . "
Mr. H. L. Wilson . . . . . . . . . . . Glassboro, N. J.
Mrs. H. L. Wilson . . . . . . . . . . "

### EXECUTIVE COMMITTEE.

C. E. Wyman, *President and Manager.*
Wm. J. Maxwell, *Secretary and Treasurer.*
George W. Brown,   John H. Reagan,
Walter W. Terry.

BROAD STREET STATION, PHILADELPHIA.

# PENNSYLVANIA RAILROAD CONDUCTORS' EXCURSION TO CALIFORNIA.

### SATURDAY, MAY 8th, 1897.

The hands on the large clock that denotes the standard time in the great corridor of Broad Street Station, Philadelphia, point to the hour 10 A. M.; an unusual commotion is noticed in the mammoth train shed, which in any hour of the day or night is filled with trains loading and discharging their cargoes of human freight, ever presenting a scene of hustling, bustling activity. The unusual commotion referred to is caused by the departure of the *Pennsylvania Railroad Conductors' Excursion to California.* Fully one thousand friends and relatives have gathered on the extensive train platform to see them off; thirty minutes of promiscuous kissing, hugging, tears, smiles, hand shaking, and good-byes, then "all aboard," and at 10.30 A. M. the five-car vestibule train rolls out over the elevated tracks bound for a journey of 9,000 miles. The notebook crank and the kodak fiend are aboard, and it is hoped that it will not be regretted that they have come. The kodak fiends are Bros. Ed. Foster, Joe Ristein, and Billy Haas, who succeed in getting some very good snaps at the train before starting, and the

Lord only knows what else was snapped at, for the snapping was kept up almost continually for the next thirty-one days. The notebook crank is the writer, who, with the ever-present notebook in hand, starts in after the train starts to make an inventory of the outfit.

The first person encountered is the good-looking and gentlemanly train conductor, W. E. Bostick, who volunteers the information that the train is running as second No. 25 over the Philadelphia Division, Philadelphia to Harrisburg; that it gives him great pleasure to run the train, for he considers it a mark of honor. We are drawn by P. R. R. engine No. 31, in charge of Engineer J. Stroh, and fired by C. B. Lewis. Next to the engine is parlor combined car No. 4808, with baggage end loaded with sixty-two pieces of baggage, two barrels, and thirty-two cases of nourishment, in charge of George H. Anderson, the colored janitor of the conductors' room in Broad Street Station, Philadelphia, who, because of his well-known character for faithfulness, honesty, and good nature, is taken along, and placed in the responsible position of baggage master and general cork extractor. The smoking end of the car is furnished with twelve movable parlor chairs and two tables, and the floor is covered with Brussels carpet. The Pullman dining car "Lafayette," in charge of Dining-car Conductor Mr. Tom McDonald, comes next.

Introducing myself to Mr. McDonald, I find him a very agreeable gentleman, who kindly gives me what information I want, also a bill of fare. The latter makes my mouth water in anticipation of what I may expect when the dinner hour arrives. This is what with keen appreciation and fast increasing appetite I read:—

## ORDER OF RAILWAY CONDUCTORS' SPECIAL.

### *EN ROUTE* TO LOS ANGELES AND RETURN.

Pullman Dining Car Service.

May 8th, 1897.

---

### DINNER.

Ox Joints.        Consomme.
Cucumbers.        Olives.
Boiled Halibut.        Egg Sauce.
Parisienne Potatoes.
Boiled Leg of Mutton.        Caper Sauce.
Apple Fritters.        Wine Sauce.
Prime Roast Beef.
Roast Long Island Spring Duck.        Apple Sauce.
Mashed Potatoes.    Boiled New Potatoes.
Boiled Onions.    Beets.    New Green Peas.
Tomato Salad au Mayonnaise.
Bread Pudding.        Cognac Sauce.
Ice Cream.    Preserved Fruits.
Assorted Cake.    Marmalade.    Dry Canton Ginger.
English and Graham Wafers.    Fruit.
Roquefort and Edam Cheese.    Bent's Biscuit.
Café Noir.

"Mr. McDonald," says I, "I do not doubt your ability to feed us as per bill of promise, but I am curious to know where you keep all this material and how you prepare it for the table?" "It is easily explained; I will show you," is the reply. "Built here in this end of the car is a large cupboard refrigerator in which can be stored a large amount of stuff, underneath the car are two large ice chests in which can be placed several hundred pounds of meat, and on top of the car you will find a large tank containing many gallons of water. In the other end of the car you will find the kitchen, where the victuals are prepared, and the sideboard containing the dishes and other ware belonging to the dining car. If it were necessary to do so, we could stock this car with material enough at one time to last a party of one hundred persons one week; but ordinarily we lay in but a limited amount, as provisions or other material is furnished as needed from the Pullman supply stations *en route*, thus we can always have it good and fresh."

"You seem to have lots of help," I remarked, as I noticed nine or ten neat, gentlemanly-looking mulattoes in their snow-white coats and aprons bustling about the car.

"Yes, I am pleased to say that you can expect excellent service from the cooks and waiters in this car. Mr. Martin and Mr. Bostwick, of the Pullman palace car service, have kindly furnished me with men of which it can be said there are no better in the service." "Can you give me their names?" "Certainly; the cooks are: *Chief*, R. W. Moore; *assistants*, H. F. Robinson, T. Allen, F. L. Litt; *waiters*, W. Hill, A. Beard, O. Fisher, C. Coleman, C. Jackson. We have ten tables in the car, each table seats four, which enables us to accommodate forty persons at a time. Each waiter has been assigned his place, knows just what he has to do, and while there may at times be a little delay in filling orders, there is never any confusion."

"There is another thing," continues Mr. McDonald, "which no doubt you will notice, and that is our strict adherence to the law of cleanliness. If there is one rule of the dining-car service more imperative than another, it is the one that declares that everything must be clean. The coats and aprons of the waiters must be pure and spotless as an angel's robe, napkins and table linen must

A PULLMAN DINING CAR.

never be used the second time, no matter how little soiled. This is a rule that at all times must be rigidly enforced, and it would cost me my situation to allow it to be violated."

Thanking Mr. McDonald for his kind information, I turn my back on the "Lafayette" for the time being, entirely convinced that a first-class fully-equipped dining car is the greatest wonder that ever went on wheels.

Next to the "Lafayette" I find the sleeper "Marco." I also find as I emerge from the narrow passageway, which is an unavoidable nuisance in all Pullman cars, the genial, good-natured, and good-looking sleeping-car conductor, Miles H. Suter, who has charge of the three Pullman sleepers that are on the train.

"Mr. Suter," I said, "the Pullman people have given us a fine train."

"Yes," he replied. "There are no more substantial or more comfortable cars in the Pullman service than these. In one of them a person can ride many hundreds of miles and not become fatigued. You will find the motion of these cars very agreeable and easy. They were selected for this trip because of this admirable qualification, and as far as ease and comfort goes I predict for your party a very pleasant tour. Another thing," continued Mr. Suter, "I have already noticed, which will contribute much to your comfort, and which is lacking in most excursion parties, is that you have plenty of room, and so are not crowded. The gentlemen who have arranged the excursion deserve a great deal of credit for the excellent judgment they have exercised in not having too many or too few, but just enough. There are no vacancies and no one is crowded. It was also wise to have no children along, for little folks often need attention that cannot be given them on a journey of this kind, and their mothers need rest instead of the worriment that comes from having the care of little ones on their hands."

"Mr. Suter," I remarked, as a genteel colored man in a neat uniform come through the car, "it must be a very laborious task when night comes for one man to convert all these seats into beds, and in the morning change them back again."

"Yes, it seems like a great deal of work, but an experienced porter will soon make the change. I have three good men, one to each car, and you have only to watch Dennis Jackson in the 'Marco,' Dick Pettus in the 'Milton,' or George Custis in the 'Orchis,' making up the berths, to be convinced that by a man who understands the business the work is more quickly and easily accomplished than one would suppose possible. Everything must be kept clean and tidy, pillow-cases and sheets changed daily, and towels used but once. Every time a towel is used a clean one takes its place. Cleanliness is an important rule in the Pullman service, and we are obliged to strictly enforce it."

Thanking Mr. Suter for his kind information I turn my attention to the occupants of the car. State room A is occupied by Conductors Suter and McDonald.

Section 1 by Mr. and Mrs. Samuel Horner. Brother Horner is a member of West Philadelphia Division No. 162, and a conductor on the New York Division. Mrs. Horner is a member of Erickson Division No. 5, L. A.

Section 2 by Colonel and Mrs. John T. Layfield. Brother Layfield is secretary and treasurer of Wilmington Division No. 224, and a conductor on the Delaware

C. E. WYMAN, CHAIRMAN OF THE COMMITTEE.

Division; he served on the staff of Governor Benjamin Biggs of Delaware several years ago, thus earning the title of colonel.

Section 3 by Mr. and Mrs. M. M. Shaw. Brother Shaw is P. C. C. of West Philadelphia Division No. 162, and a conductor on the Central Division.

Section 4 by Mr. and Mrs. Charles E. Wyman. Brother Wyman is a member of Wilmington Division No. 224, and a conductor on the Maryland Division; he is president and manager of the excursion and has worked to make it a success.

Section 5 by Mr. and Mrs. John A Reilly. Brother Reilly is a member of West Philadelphia Division No. 162, and a conductor on the Maryland Division. Mrs. Reilly is a member of Erickson Division No. 5, L. A.

Section 6 by Mr. and Mrs. William J. Maxwell. Brother Maxwell is a member of West Philadelphia Division No. 162, and a conductor on the New York Division; he is secretary and treasurer of 162, also of the excursion, and works hard in the interest of the same. Mrs. Maxwell is a member of Erickson Division No. 5, L. A.

Section 7 by Mr. and Mrs. Charles L. Springer. Brother Springer is a member of West Philadelphia Division No. 162, and a conductor on the Philadelphia Division. Mrs. Springer is a member of Erickson Division No. 5, L. A.

Section 8 by Mr. and Mrs. George W. Brown. Brother Brown is A. C. C. and a trustee of West Philadelphia Division No. 162; he is a member of the excursion executive committee, and has the welfare of the party at heart. Mrs. Brown is a member and president of Erickson Division No. 5, L. A.

Section 9 by Mr. and Mrs. George W. Dale. Brother Dale is a member of West Philadelphia Division No. 162, and a conductor on the New York Division.

Section 10 by Mr. and Mrs. Walter W. Terry. Brother Terry is a conductor on the New York Division, and a member and trustee of West Philadelphia Division No. 162; he is a member of the excursion executive committee, the heavyweight of the party, whose herculean strength and sound judgment can always be relied upon.

Section 11 by Mr. and Mrs. James M. Matthews. Brother Matthews is a member and a P. C. C. Conductor of West Philadelphia Division No. 162, and a conductor on the Schuylkill Division.

Section 12 by Brothers John H. Reagan and Charles J. McCarty. Brother Reagan is a member of West Philadelphia Division No. 162, and a conductor on the Maryland Division; he is a member of the excursion executive committee, and is keenly alive to all that pertains to the welfare and pleasure of the party. Brother McCarty is a member of Susquehanna Division No. 331, and a conductor on the Frederick Division. Brothers Reagan and McCarty enjoy the freedom of bachelorship, and are general favorites with the ladies.

Drawing room 13 is occupied by Colonel and Mrs. Mitchell. Brother Mitchell is a member of West Philadelphia Division No. 162, and a conductor on the Maryland Division; he is well known as a genial, good-hearted fellow, and was given the title of "Colonel" several years ago by his associates because of his entertaining and hospitable disposition.

Leaving the "Marco" with its happy occupants, whose comforts will be looked after by the polite and attentive porter, Dennis Jackson, I passed through the vestibule into the next car, "Milton," which I found similar in almost every respect to the "Marco." Meeting the porter, stalwart, good-natured Dick Pettus, I informed him that I had visited the "Milton" in order to obtain the position and names of the occupants.

"I'm not much acquainted with anybody yet," replied Dick, "but don't think I'll have any trouble, as everybody seems to be all right and happy."

"Yes," I answered, as I took a glance at the occupants of the car, "you will find them all first rate people, and all right in the daytime, but be careful and keep the doors locked and your eye on them at night, for there are two or three in this car who are afflicted with somnambulism, and they might walk off the train or get into the wrong berth while in such a condition." "Good Lord," was Dick's reply as he vanished into the toilet room. I find the state room in the "Milton" reserved for a hospital. It is hoped it will not be needed for such a purpose.

Section 1 is occupied by Mr. and Mrs. J. W. Goff. Brother Goff is a member of Camden Division No. 170, and a conductor on the West Jersey and Seashore Division.

Section 2 by Mr. and Mrs. H. L. Wilson. Brother Wilson is a member of Camden Division No. 170, and a conductor on the West Jersey and Seashore Division.

Section 3 by Mr. and Mrs. Thomas B. Gilliland. Brother Gilliland is a member of Dauphin Division No. 143, and a conductor on the Middle Division. Mrs. Gilliland is a member of Keystone Division No. 47, L. A.

Section 4 by Mr. and Mrs. L. E. Sheppard. Brother Sheppard is a member of Camden Division No. 170, and a yardmaster on the Amboy Division. Mrs. Sheppard is a member of Erickson Division No. 5, L. A.

Section 5 by Mr. and Mrs. S. N. Kilgore. Brother Kilgore is a member of West Philadelphia Division No. 162, and a conductor on the Philadelphia Division.

Section 6, Mr. and Mrs. D. R. Sparks. Brother Sparks is a member of Camden Division No. 170, and a conductor on the West Jersey Division.

Section 7 by Mr. and Mrs. E. A. Kalkman. Brother Kalkman is a member of Capitol Division No. 378, and a conductor on the Maryland Division.

Section 8 by Mr. and Mrs. W. H. Morris. Brother Morris is a member of Wilmington Division No. 224, and a conductor on the Maryland Division.

Section 9 by Mr. and Mrs. C. E. Foster. Brother Foster is a member of West Philadelphia Division No. 162, and a conductor on the Maryland Division.

Section 10 by Mr. and Mrs. I. M. Cohee. Brother Cohee is a member of Wilmington Division No. 224, and a conductor on the Maryland Division.

Section 11 by Mr. and Mrs. James Dougherty. Brother Dougherty is a member of West Philadelphia Division No. 162, and a conductor on the New York Division.

Section 12 by Mr. and Mrs. James H. Moore. Brother Moore is a member of West Philadelphia Division No. 162, and a conductor on the New York Division.

Drawing room by Doctor and Mrs. C. E. Mattson. Brother Mattson is a member of West Philadelphia Division No. 162, and a conductor on the Maryland Division; he is a graduate of Jefferson Medical College, and has quite an extensive practice, to which he devotes his time when not engaged in his duties on the road.

A PULLMAN SLEEPING CAR.

Brother Mattson has kindly consented to give the party his professional care while on the trip, if needed, but it is earnestly hoped that there will be but a very few occasions for an exercise of his professional skill and that his labors in this direction will be light.

Entering the "Orchis," the fifth and last car on the train, I found the polite and obliging porter, George Custis, busily engaged in the duties pertaining to his position. His passengers all looked comfortable and George looked happy.

"George, do you like fun?" I quietly asked as he passed near me to deposit a huge telescope valise in the state room. "Yes, sir; somewhat," he replied, with a questioning look in his eye. "You will have a circus on your hands, my boy, or I fail to read the combination," I added, as he emerged from the state room. I had glanced down the line as I entered the car and noticed among the occupants some well-known characters for fun and frolic, and conclude there is a picnic in store for the porter and passengers of the sleeper "Orchis."

Turning now to the business that brought me to the "Orchis," I find that the state room is occupied by Messrs. Charles Sloane and William Haas. Brother Sloane is a member of Quaker City Division No. 204, and a conductor on the Philadelphia Division; he is the *Nimrod* of the party, and has come equipped with fishing tackle and rifle. He is well acquainted with some of the best hunting grounds in the West, and is familiar with the haunts and habits of bear and deer. Brother Haas is a member of R. B. Hawkins Division No. 114, and a conductor on West Penn Division; he has a kodak with which he expects to secure some interesting views.

Brothers Sloane and Haas enjoy the privileges and liberties of single-blessedness, but are not averse to the society of ladies.

Section 1 by Messrs. Joseph Schuler and John B. Crispen. Brother Schuler is a member of R. B. Hawkins Division No. 114, and a conductor on the Pittsburgh Division. Brother Crispen is secretary and treasurer of Renovo Division No. 333, and a conductor on the Middle Division, Philadelphia and Erie Railroad. He is a bachelor, young in years, and inclined to be shy in the presence of the ladies.

Section 2 by Messrs. T. J. Denniston and J. J. Restein. Brother Denniston is a member of West Philadelphia Division No. 162, and a conductor on the New York Division; he is a bachelor, arrived at the years of discretion, cautious and modest in his habits, an excellent conversationalist, whose companionship is appreciated and enjoyed by all. Brother Restein is a member of Wilmington Division No. 224, and a conductor on the New York, Philadelphia and Norfolk Railroad. He keeps his kodak always handy, for it is his purpose to try to obtain some of the best views of incidents and scenery on the trip.

Section 3 by Mr. and Mrs. Robert T. Elder. Brother Elder is a member of West Philadelphia Division No. 162, and a conductor on the New York Division.

Section 4 by Mr. and Mrs. Hugh Leary. Brother Leary is a member of West Philadelphia Division No. 162, and a conductor on the Schuylkill Division; he has been but a few days married, and both bride and groom receive the congratulation of many friends in being so fortunate as to be able to take such an enjoyable wedding tour. May sunshine, health, and happiness be ever theirs.

Section 5 by Mr. P. J. Barrett and his sister, Miss Anna S. Barrett. Brother Barrett is a member of West Philadelphia Division No. 162, and a conductor on the New York Division. Being a single man, he had no wife to accompany him, but he did the next best thing and brought his sister, a commendable act that redounds to Brother Barrett's credit. A man that is good to his sister will be good to a wife. Mark it!

Section 6, Mr. William H. Post and daughter, Miss Ella L. Post. Brother Post is a member of West Philadelphia Division No. 162, and a conductor on the New York Division. Mrs. Post being unable, on account of ill health, to accompany the excursion, permitted her daughter to take her place, a privilege the young lady highly appreciates and enjoys.

Section 7, Mr. and Mrs. J. N. Climenson. Brother Climenson is a member of West Philadelphia Division No. 162, and a conductor on the Philadelphia Division.

Section 8, Mr. and Mrs. R. J. Foulon. Brother Foulon is a member and P. C. C. of Quaker City Division No. 204, and a conductor on the Philadelphia Division.

Section 9, Mr. and Mrs. H. R. Haefner. Brother Haefner is C. C. of Susquehanna Division No. 331, and a conductor on the Philadelphia Division.

Section 10, Mr. and Mrs. C. F. Smith. Brother Smith is a member of Susquehanna Division No. 331, and a conductor on the Frederick Division.

Section 11, Mr. and Mrs. T. J. McKernan. Brother McKernan is a member of Neptune Division No. 169, and assistant passenger yardmaster at Jersey City.

Section 12, Mr. and Mrs. M. Houston. Brother Houston is S. C. of West Philadelphia Division No. 162, and a conductor on the Schuylkill Division. Mrs. Houston is a member of Erickson Division No. 5, L. A.

Drawing room, Messrs. C. E. Waddington, O. Williams, and H. H. Taylor. Brother Waddington is C. C. of West Philadelphia Division No. 162, and a conductor on the New York Division; Brother Williams is a member of West Philadelphia Division No. 162, and a conductor on the Maryland Division; Brother Taylor is a member of West Philadelphia Division No. 162, and a conductor on the New York Division. Brothers Waddington and Williams are unmarried, but it is not known for how long. We can only wait and see.

On the rear platform stood Brakeman T. M. Tobin, who was selected by Trainmaster Simms to accompany Conductor Bostick as flagman because of his well-known adherence to the rules that govern this important position. We are spinning along at about a fifty mile per hour rate of speed, and have passed through some of the finest farming country in the world. A "fleeting view" is all we get, but one glance is sufficient to show us fine, substantial buildings and fences in good repair and men busily engaged in preparing the soil for the reception of seed.

We have passed the city of Lancaster and are nearing Harrisburg. Dinner has been announced, and I retrace my steps to the dining car to find the tables filled. Although hungry I console myself with the thought that "there are others, lots of others," and that in my misery I had lots of company. In the meantime I avail myself of the opportunity of ascertaining who our guests are, as a number of gentlemen accompanied us from Philadelphia.

Glancing up the line of tables, I see Trainmasters Frank Carlisle of the Maryland, James G. Ruth of the Central, Walter B. Gormley of the Schuylkill, and Rees L. Hannum of the Delaware Extension and Kensington Divisions; Yardmasters L. H. Smith, Kensington, and Anthony Hughes, Fifteenth and Washington Avenue, and George Stults, assistant secretary of West Philadelphia Division No. 162. They seem to be having a good time, and are all bravely battling with Jersey mutton and Long Island spring duck.

In the centre of one of the tables is a magnificent bouquet of choice flowers, presented to the party in Philadelphia by Messrs. Myers & Lautman, florists, of Wyndmoor, Chestnut Hill. It is much admired by all for its beauty and fragrance. As the tables became vacant they were rapidly filled up by those in waiting, and it was not long until the entire party had partaken of a dinner that was admitted by all to be hard to beat, and a credit to Conductor McDonald and his competent and obliging help.

At 1.22 P. M. we arrived at Harrisburg, where a short stop of eight minutes was made in changing engines. We bid adieu to our guests, receiving from them many congratulations and compliments as to our outfit and prospects, and best wishes for a happy trip and safe return. The jovial trainmaster of the Central Division, as he bade us goodbye, said: "You people could not travel in better form or fare better if you were a party of millionaires. I am sure you will have a good time."

Whole-souled, big-hearted Frank Carlisle heaved a

great sigh as he shook hands with Manager Wyman and Colonel Mitchell, and with a tear in his eye murmured, "Boys, I wish I could go with you." Walt Gormley and George Stults turned their backs on the crowd to hide their emotion as "all aboard" rang out, and the last seen of "Tony" Hughes he was struggling in the grasp of Lew Smith and Rees Hannum, who had to hold him to prevent him from boarding the now fast-receding train, they knowing full well that business at Fifteenth and Washington Avenue would suffer did they not take "Tony" back with them.

It was just 1.30 P. M. when we left Harrisburg, drawn by P. R. R. engine No. 32, handled by Engineer John Ficks and fired by Jesse Reynolds. Conductor A. W. Black had charge of the train from Harrisburg to Altoona, with Flagman J. S. Wagner and Brakeman A. Gable. W. Brooke Moore, trainmaster of the Middle Division, was a guest on the train from Harrisburg to Altoona. We arrived at Altoona 4.50 P. M. and left at 4.57 P. M. with P. R. R. engine No. 867, Engineer F. W. Masterson, Fireman E. W. Pugh, Conductor W. B. Chislett, Flagman Frank Bollinger, Brakemen John Cline and C. D. Chamberlain. As guests we had C. W. Culp, trainmaster Pittsburgh Division, and D. M. Perine, assistant master mechanic, of Altoona, who accompanied the party to Pittsburgh.

Six miles west of Altoona we reach Kittanning Point and circle round the famous Horseshoe Curve. From this point a magnificent view of Alleghany Mountain scenery can be seen. Nine miles further and we reach the highest elevation on our trip across the Alleghanies and pass Cresson, a beautiful summer resort, the loca-

SANG HOLLOW ON THE CONEMAUGH.

tion of the noted "Mountain House," whose marvelous reputation for rates and rations attracts the *bon-ton* patronage of the world.

We now enter the Conemaugh country and note its picturesque hills and mountain ridges, among which winds and wriggles the historic Conemaugh River, which at present seems but little more than a harmless, babbling brook; but when the rains fall and the snows melt, and this sparkling little creek receives the waters from a hundred hills, it becomes a very demon in its resistless fury. For eight miles we have followed this stream and part company with it as we pass through the city of Johnstown. Johnstown will ever remember the Conemaugh River, flowing as it does through the very centre of the city. It is a constant menace to the tranquillity and security of the people, and in yonder hillside cemetery two thousand glistening tombstones bear sad and silent testimony to the awful horrors of a Conemaugh flood.

It has grown dark and we are approaching Pittsburgh. A stop is made at East Liberty, and a delegation of brothers from R. B. Hawkins Division No. 114 of Pittsburgh get aboard and accompany us into Pittsburgh. The visitors kindly present each one of our party with a bouquet of roses. We arrive at Pittsburgh 8.12 P. M. and stop for eighteen minutes, leaving at 8.30 (7.30 Central) P. M. Time changes now from Eastern to Central, which makes us leave at 7.30 instead of 8.30. To some of us this is rather a perplexing thing, for we are leaving Pittsburgh forty-two minutes before we arrive there. A number of our party are setting their watches to Central time, I will allow mine to remain as it is, and will use Eastern time in my notes in connection with the Standard time of whatever locality we may be in.

Left Pittsburgh with P. C. C. & St. L. engine No. 183, Engineer A. F. Winchell, Fireman O. Brown, who runs us to Dennison, Ohio, 93 miles. Conductor L. E. Schull, Brakemen W. A. Chambers and E. S. Chambers go with us to Columbus, Ohio, 193 miles. We almost regret that it is night, for we desire to see the country. At 9.50 (8.50 Central) P. M. we arrive at Steubenville, 43 miles from Pittsburgh, and stop five minutes for water.

We are now on the Pittsburgh Division of the Pennsylvania lines, operated by the Pittsburgh, Cincinnati, Chicago and St. Louis Railway Company. The Pittsburgh Division extends from Pittsburgh, Pa., to Columbus, Ohio, a distance of 193 miles. Most of the party have turned in and at 11.30 (10.30 Central), just as our train stops at Dennison, Ohio, I prepare to undertake the novel experiment of trying to get a night's sleep in the berth of a Pullman car. It is a new and strange experience to me, but I go at it to win. There is nobody in sight, but the presence of a carload of people is felt. The long, narrow aisle of the car is deserted, but I hesitate to exercise the privilege its deserted condition would seem to warrant. I desire to undress, but I wish to hide to do it, and with this end in view I crawl under the curtains that inclose our berth. As I do so the train starts on its way again. Mrs. S. has retired some time ago, and I think is asleep. There is not much room for me, but I determine to make the best of it. Balancing myself on the edge of the berth, I make a few changes in my apparel, and come very near being precipitated into the aisle while so doing by a sudden lurch of the car as the train struck a curve. In regaining my equilibrium I stepped upon the madam, who quietly inquired what I was trying to do. "Only coming to bed, my dear," I answered. "Is that all," she replied, "I have been watching you for some time and thought you either had a fit or else was practicing gymnastics and using the curtain pole for a horizontal bar." I made no reply, I didn't blame her, and lay down thankful that she was the only witness to the performance; and ours was not the only circus on the train that night; "there were others."

## SUNDAY, MAY 9th.

Got up early, after passing rather a restless night; did not sleep very well; finished dressing just as the train stops at Richmond, Ind., 5.55 (4.55 Central) A. M. Go outside and find it a lovely morning. Several of the boys are up. Have come 220 miles since I turned in last night as the train left Dennison, Ohio.

We are now on the Indianapolis Division of the Pittsburgh, Cincinnati, Chicago and St. Louis Railway, which runs from Columbus, Ohio, to Indianapolis, Ind., a distance of 188 miles. Upon inquiry I learn that from Dennison to Columbus we had P. C. C. & St. L. engine No. 59, Engineer Schultz. From Columbus to Indianapolis, P. C. C. & St. L. engine No. 102, Engineer John Cassell, Fireman W. Mason, Conductor J. E. Taylor, Brakemen Orvil Hyer and George Farmer. We arrive at Indianapolis 7.45 (6.45 Central) A. M., and leave there at 8.30 (7.30 Central) A. M. on the Main Line Division of the Vandalia Line, which extends from Indianapolis to St. Louis, a distance of 240 miles, and is controlled and operated by the Terre Haute and Indianapolis Railroad Company. T. H. & I. engine No. 34 is drawing us. It is called the World's Fair engine, having been built at Pittsburgh and placed on exhibition at Chicago during the great exposition. It is a fine, large engine, and Engineer Fred. Wood, who runs it, says "she is a daisy." The fireman is G. E. Hickman; conductor, A. J. Harshman; brakemen, J. G. McMahon and James Edmunds. Breakfast is announced as we leave Indianapolis, and no second invitation is required; our appetites are keen, and we thoroughly enjoy McDonald's substantial and bountiful breakfast.

We pass through Terre Haute at 10.15 (9.15 Central) A. M., and cross the Wabash River a short distance west of the city. Ten minutes after passing through Terre Haute we cross the State line and enter Illinois. There is a delay of five minutes at Effingham by a hot box on engine 34. Just after leaving Effingham a stone was thrown by some one and broke an outside window in car "Milton," section 4, occupied by Mr. and Mrs. L. E. Sheppard. A stop of five minutes is made at Greenville to oil and take water. Three strange men boarded the train at this point and were not noticed until after it had started, when they claimed they had made a mistake, thinking it a regular train. The train was stopped to leave them off. We partook of lunch at 1.15 (12.15 Central) P. M., being always ready to eat.

It is raining as we approach St. Louis, where we arrive at 2.30 (1.30 Central) P. M. The effects of last Summer's terrible tornado can plainly be seen, as we cross the bridge from East St. Louis, in great piles of *débris* that have not as yet been cleared away. On account of the rain the prospect of seeing much of the city is very poor. A trolley ride of five miles through the city to Forrest Park was taken by a number of our party. It is too wet to take a walk in the park, and after spending a half hour in a large pavilion watching the pouring rain we return to the Union Depot, which we look through and find it to be a large and magnificent structure, exceeding in size and excelling in grandeur our own Broad Street Station at Philadelphia. It was built at an expense of $6,500,000, and covers an area of 424,200 square feet. The train shed contains thirty tracks, which are used by twenty-two different roads.

Several of us met Conductor W. Fetzer, of the Louisville and Nashville, and had a pleasant half hour with him. On account of a defective flange, a pair of new wheels were put under the dining car "Lafayette" this afternoon. Mrs. Shaw, Mrs. Dale, Mrs. Reilly, and Miss Post are on the sick list this afternoon. Called to dinner at 8.30 (7.30 Central) P. M., after which we were escorted through the magnificent station by Stationmaster J. J. Coakley and Conductor A. J. Harshman. The station is lighted with thousands of electric lights of many different hues and colors. Every light is burning to-night, the second time since the construction of the station, the first time at its dedication, September 1st, 1894, and this the second time in honor of the visit of the Pennsylvania Railroad conductors, May 9th, 1897. Our most sincere thanks are due the kind and courteous stationmaster, J. J. Coakley, for the favor and honor accorded us. May his shadow never grow less.

An itinerary souvenir of our train over the Iron Mountain Route, Texas and Pacific and Southern Pacific Railways, from St. Louis to Los Angeles, via Texarkana and El Paso, was presented to each member of our party by the Iron Mountain Route management through Mr. Coakley. It is a neat little affair, much appreciated, and will be highly prized as a souvenir of our trip.

At 9.15 (8.15 Central) P. M. our train rolled out of the Grand Union Depot over the Iron Mountain Route, which extends from St. Louis to Texarkana, a distance of 490 miles. St. L. I. M. & S. engine No. 630 is drawing us, with Engineer John Hayes at the throttle, Fireman J. E. Schader, Conductor W. Hall, Brakeman J. L. Thompson, and Baggagemaster M. Madison. We have this engine and crew to Poplar Bluff, 166 miles, with the exception of the baggagemaster, who goes through to Texarkana. There is an inquiry for Brother Reagan; he has not been seen since leaving St. Louis. Our hearts are filled with consternation and alarm, for we believe he has been left, and how can we get along without "Jack; good, jolly, jovial Jack." Maxwell's eyes are dimmed with tears of sorrow, and McCarty is wringing his hands in grief. "Let us stop the train and return and get him," suggested Mrs. Kalkman. "I believe he has been kidnaped," said Brother Sloane, "or he would never have got left." "He's all right; I found him," shouted Brother Waddington, as he entered the car, and there was great rejoicing when it was learned that instead of being kidnaped and left behind, Brother Reagan was peacefully sleeping in Brother Waddington's berth in the drawing room in rear of the train.

F. B. DeGarmo, trainmaster of St. Louis, Iron Mount-

AT EFFINGHAM, ILLINOIS.

LEAVING LONGVIEW JUNCTION, TEXAS.

ain and Southern Railroad, and his assistant, T. H. Gray, accompanied us from St. Louis to Poplar Bluff, and Conductor P. Elkins, a member of DeSoto Division No. 241, got on at DeSoto and went with us to Bismarck. A large number of our party were gathered in the smoking car and we had quite an entertainment. Brother Elkins sang a number of songs, and the cook and waiters, one of them having a banjo, entertained us with songs and music hard to beat, and most thoroughly enjoyed by all. Conductors McDonald and Suter and Brother Haas sang excellent songs, and Wyman and Shaw gave recitations. Our genial train conductor, Capt. W. Hall, related some interesting stories of the days when this section of the country was terrorized by the operations and exploits of the Jesse James' gang of train robbers. Captain Hall's train was held up one night by this daring band of thieves at Gad's Hill, 120 miles south of St. Louis. Hall was forced to surrender and remain quiet with the cold muzzle of a revolver pressed against his temple. An attempt was made to blow open the safe in the express car, but the robbers became frightened at their own noise and fled without securing any booty. The evening has been such a very enjoyable one that midnight approaches unawares; finding it so late we turn in, having less difficulty in doing so than we had last night.

## MONDAY, MAY 10th.

Got up this morning at 6.30 (5.30 Central) and found our train in charge of Conductor H. C. Withrow and Engineer A. B. Archibald, with St. L. I. M. & S. engine No. 375, fired by T. Grifin. Captain Withrow took charge of the train at Poplar Bluff, with instructions to consume ten hours and thirty-two minutes in the run to Texarkana, a distance of 325 miles. Withrow has no brakeman, but is accompanied by a colored porter, J. J. Norris, who performs the duties of a brakeman. We are now in Arkansas, having crossed the State line last night at Moark, 185 miles south of St. Louis. We arrive at Little Rock, Ark., 8.15 (7.15 Central) A. M., and make a stop of ten minutes. We alight to look around and very much admire the "375," and are informed that it is one of the best engines on the Iron Mountain Route and the first one built at the company's new shops at Baring Cross, Little Rock, Ark. Went to breakfast at 9.10 (8.10 Central), hungry as a hyena.

We cannot help but notice as we journey through Arkansas the advanced condition of vegetation. Farmers in the East are only preparing their ground for corn, and here it is up; potatoes are in blossom, and peas are ready for use. Cotton is grown extensively here, and many acres are seen with the plants just peeping through the ground. We are now nearing the southern extremity of the State and approaching Texarkana, where we arrive at 12.35 (11.35 A. M. Central) P. M., having passed through the State of Arkansas 305 miles in a slightly southwesterly direction.

A stop of twenty-five minutes is given us at Texarkana, which is on the line between Arkansas and Texas, one-half of the station being in Arkansas and the other half in Texas. Brother Wyman, who acts in the double capacity of manager and clown, has a robe of crazy patchwork design, a veritable coat of many colors, in which he has arrayed himself, much to the amusement

AT FORT WORTH, TEXAS.

of the crowd of natives who have assembled on our arrival. The antics of Brother Wyman and a number of others who have taken possession of a bronco and a team of donkeys occasion a great deal of merriment. As we are about to leave, Mrs. Robert Foulon was presented with a large bunch of beautiful magnolias by her friend, Mrs. Carmichael, of Texarkana. It graced the sideboard of the dining car for many days and was much admired.

Left Texarkana 1.35 (12.35 Central) P. M. on the Texas and Pacific Road, with T. & P. engine No. 126, Engineer William Gunn, Conductor Joseph Scully, Brakeman J. C. Smith, who will run us to Longview Junction, 97 miles. E. W. Campbell, trainmaster on the Eastern Division of the Texas and Pacific, will go with us to Fort Worth, the terminus of his division, 253 miles. Trainmaster Campbell is a member of Alamo Division No. 59, of Texarkana. Brother Sloane went to a barber shop in Texarkana and got left. Trainmaster Campbell left instructions for the conductor of the following train to carry him to Longview Junction, where he will overtake us. No "weeping and wailing and gnashing of teeth" in this case, for we are assured of the safety of our brother.

We arrived at Longview Junction on time, 5.22 (4.22 Central) P. M., and five minutes later the following train, No. 55, arrived and with it came Brother Sloane, who was given quite a reception, the ladies presenting him with bouquets of natural grasses and flowers and the "boys" tying a cord to him and leading him into the train. He has promised not to do it again.

Our train was attached to No. 55, which is called the

"Cannon Ball" Express, and at 5.35 (4.35 Central) P. M. we left Longview Junction with a train of nine cars, drawn by T. & P. engine No. 229, in charge of Engineer E. Smith, fired by S. Jones; Conductor E. R. Woodward, Porter and Brakeman Bristoe Young, who ran us to Fort Worth, a distance of 156 miles, where we arrive 11.20 (10.20 Central) P. M. Just before reaching the city we cross the Trinity River.

When we arrive at Fort Worth we learn that there is trouble ahead of us somewhere, caused by high water, which has a discouraging effect. We will lay over at this point to-night, with the expectation of learning more in the morning. There is a heavy thunder storm and it is raining hard as we turn in at 11.30 (10.30 Central) P. M.

### TUESDAY, MAY 11th.

Got up at 6.30 (5.30 Central), and found it raining hard. It cleared up about eight o'clock and the party started out to see the town, it having been announced that our train would leave at 12.15 (11.15 A. M. Central) P. M., nothing definite having been learned as to the trouble ahead. Our party received the best of treatment from the good people of the town, and many places of interest were visited. Officer H. C. Town, of the city police, loaded sixteen of the party in a patrol wagon and drove through the city to the City Hall, where they were kindly received and shown over the building, from there to the water works, and through the park to a point where a trolley line took them to the station. It was a very enjoyable trip. Others of our party visited other places of interest and had equally as good a time. A

Yours in P.F.
O. H. Bacon
J-P Ry

number of souvenirs were procured, the most highly prized being the Texan sunbonnets, which so fascinated the ladies of our party that they purchased, it is said, all that were on sale in the city. They are very unique in style and worn very extensively by the native women of this locality. Brother Post purchased a Texan sombrero, and all agree that it is very becoming; the ladies are wearing their sunbonnets; Wyman has his circus gown and a Texan sunbonnet on; and a photographer is placing his apparatus in position to take a snap at the train and party before we leave. With the snap of the camera comes the shout of "all aboard," and as we scamper on, the train moves slowly off, and we leave Fort Worth behind us, but carry away with us pleasant memories of the beauty of the city and of the kindness and civility of its people.

T. & P. engine No. 188, run by Engineer John Baker and fired by John Price, draws our train from Fort Worth to Big Springs, a distance of 270 miles. Conductor O. H. Bacon and Brakeman Charles Gunning go with us from Fort Worth to El Paso, a distance of 616 miles. Division Superintendent J. B. Paul accompanied us from Fort Worth to Weatherford, 31 miles. Shortly after leaving Weatherford we crossed the Brazos River and obtained a fine view of the Brazos Mountains. As we passed Eastland, 105 miles west of Fort Worth, we noticed devastation and ruin, the effect, we were told, of a recent cyclone. A few miles further we reach Baird and stop ten minutes for orders and water. A little boy about three years of age attracts the attention of some of our party, who ascertain that his name is Reynaud Strobe; his mother and grandfather live at the station;

his father, who was an employe of the railroad, was killed in an accident about a year ago, almost in sight of his home. Master Reynaud is taken through the train and his little cap is filled with cake and coin and his infant mind with wonderment and awe. He cannot understand it, and his baby face expresses the puzzled condition of his mind. Should he live it is hoped he will remember the *Pennsylvania Railroad Conductors' Excursion.*

We have now entered the plains of Texas and at 6.20 (5.20 Central) P. M. commence to pass through the prairie dog district. Brother Post is at the throttle; he ran No. 188 for about 50 miles and claims to have killed two jack rabbits and a prairie dog. Jack rabbits and prairie dogs are very numerous through this section, and can be seen scampering in all directions as the train thunders past. We are now nearing Big Springs, where a stop will be made to change engines. It has become dark, and we can no longer view the landscape, jack rabbits, and prairie dogs. We arrive at Big Springs 10.15 (9.15 Central) P. M., and after a delay of fifteen minutes leave with T. & P. engine No. 75, manned by Engineer D. C. Everley and Fireman Lewis Lem, whose run extends to El Paso, 347 miles. We have now entered the Great Staked Plains, and regretting that the darkness prevents us from seeing this famous country, we retire for the night at 12.20 (11.20 P. M. Central) A. M.

## WEDNESDAY, MAY 12th.

Turned out this morning about the usual time, and found the train standing at San Martine Station, 174 miles east of El Paso. As we move on our way again we find we are passing through a picturesque, but barren

A GROUP AT VAN HORN, TEXAS.

TOM McDONALD AND FRED BEACH.

country of plains and mountain ranges. A run of 50 miles from San Martine brings us to Van Horn, where we make a halt of forty-five minutes and are entertained by Mrs. M. R. Beach and her son Fred. Mrs. Beach has charge of the station at Van Horn, which is also a supply station for the railroad. Fred. is a young man about twenty-five years old, and a veritable cowboy both in appearance and deportment. He entertained and amused the party with an exhibition of bronco riding, and to show his skill in the use of the lasso, chased Brother Wyman and lassoed him with the bronco at a full run. Miss Myrtle Taylor, a young lady who is visiting Mrs. Beach, also rode the bronco for the amusement of the party, but it was noticed that the animal exhibited a far more gentle spirit under the young lady's management than it did when in charge of Fred. A cyclone cellar in the back yard was an object of much interest, and the interior was explored by several of the party. All the dwellings, of which there are but few through this region, we are told, have their cyclone pits. For many miles through this country there are no habitations except along the line of the railroad, and the people are all employes of the Texas and Pacific Railroad Company.

Leaving Van Horn, we pass close to the Sierra Blanca Mountain range, and in a short time stop at Sierra Blanca, where we lay over for half an hour and devote the time to looking around. Sierra Blanca is 92 miles southeast of El Paso and is the conjunction of the Texas and Pacific and Southern Pacific Railroads, which use joint tracks from this point to El Paso. A number of us visited the adobe residence of Jacob Hand, an aged miner and prospector, who kindly allowed us to inspect his dwelling, which is a very unique and novel affair, a part of which is used for a school, and the old gentleman is the teacher. Mr. Hand generously gave our party specimens of gold, silver, and copper ore, which are highly prized as souvenirs. Brother Haas had considerable difficulty in getting in range of the old gentleman with his kodak, but succeeded by strategy in getting a "snap" before we left; also one of a group of the party with the dwelling in the background. In the midst of the group is seen a Mexican babe held in the arms of one of the ladies of the party, who is closely watched by the mother of the infant, who fears her babe will be appropriated for a souvenir.

Leaving Sierra Blanca, we pass in sight and within about 20 miles of Livermore's Peak, 8200 feet high, said to be the highest point in Texas. We have now entered a wild, barren, broken, uninhabited region, hemmed in by dreary, ominous-looking mountain ranges. As the road traverses this broken, desolate district, there are places where almost complete circles are made in order to avoid ridges and ravines. Just after passing Malone Station, 15 miles from Sierra Blanca, we encounter a curve, and after following the circle for over a mile, find the tracks are less than 200 yards apart.

Mrs. Wyman, Mrs. Layfield, Mrs. Shaw, Brother Layfield, and myself rode on the engine from Finlay to Ft. Hancock, which afforded us a fine view of the rugged scenery through which we passed. We arrived at washout, 5 miles east of El Paso, at 5.30 (4.30 Central) P. M., and find our train can proceed no further until the track is repaired, four miles of it at the present time being under water.

MYRTLE TAYLOR ON A BRONCO.

RESIDENCE OF JACOB HAND, SIERRA BLANCA, TEXAS.

Wagons were in waiting to convey the party six miles across a desert plateau to El Paso at one dollar per head; all but a few took advantage of this method of reaching the city. The remembrance of this ride will not fade from the memory in a hurry—six miles of knee-deep, red-hot desert, dust and sand, through which the horses could scarcely drag their loads. We have a good view of the flooded district and notice many buildings surrounded with water, the occupants of which were forced to flee to higher ground. All this water, we are told, is the result of melting snows away up in the mountain districts, 75 or 80 miles away. There is seldom any rain through this region, and the Rio Grande, one half the year a shallow, insignificant stream, is to-day spread over many miles of country, causing devastation, ruin, and suffering.

Arriving in the city of El Paso, we are obliged to seek for accommodations, which causes a separation of our party. The Firemen's State Convention is in progress here, and the town is full of visitors. Ten of us found rooms at the "Grand Central," some at "Vendome," and a number at the "Pierson." The latter is the most popular place, and an effort was made to get the entire party quartered there, but it could not be done. After engaging rooms at the "Grand Central" we went across the river, which is not overflowed at this point, into the old Mexican town of Ciudad Juarez, the Paso del Norte of our childhood geographies.

Under the escort of Conductors T. H. Purcell and Charles Allen, of the Southern Pacific, we were shown much that was of interest. We were introduced by Captain Purcell to Signor Miguel Ahuamada, the gentlemanly Governor of the State of Chihuahua, who entertained us very nicely for half an hour, giving us an international treat, which ceremony consists of drinks of whatever each member of the party wishes, the guests forming in a semicircle in front of the Governor, touching glasses with him as they pass. Captain Purcell at the same time made a speech in the Mexican language, with which he is thoroughly conversant, having at one time filled the position of Government Interpreter at this point. Of course none of us understood a thing that he said, but we felt sure it was all right from the pleased expression on his Honor's face, who replied in a pleasant manner in his native tongue.

Purcell told us afterward that he had informed the Governor that we were a party of Americans who had called to do him honor; that we drank to his health and a long and happy life; that we had the highest regard for Mexican institutions, believing them to be the best in the world; that their men were the noblest and their women the most beautiful we had ever met; that we wore upon our bosoms the colors of the Mexican flag, which we considered, next to the Stars and Stripes, the most beautiful banner in the world, and we hoped it would ever wave in triumph and in peace over an empire that would continue to increase in prosperity and wealth. No wonder the old man smiled; we would have smiled too had we understood what was being said. The red, white and green of our tourist badges had caught his eye and he was pleased. Captain Purcell's speech flatters him and he wants to do something to show his appreciation.

Our visit does him great honor, and he desires to reciprocate; had he time to arrange for a bull fight he could give us much amusement, but his best bull was killed a short time ago and his matadors are out of training; but he has a prisoner under the sentence of death, and if we will return on the morrow he will execute him for our pleasure and entertainment. Captain Purcell made us acquainted with this proposition, which we declined with thanks. We had no desire to see the poor fellow shot, which is their method of administering capital punishment. Bidding his Honor adieu, we are next escorted through several of the principal gambling resorts and are much interested in all we see. It is growing late, and when we return to El Paso and reach our rooms it is midnight.

## THURSDAY, MAY 13th.

Arose about 6.30 and found the morning clear and warm. There are many wonderful, strange, and unusual things in, around, and about El Paso, but one of the most puzzling and perplexing things is its time. Traveling westward you arrive on Central time and depart on Pacific, a difference of two hours, while in the city they use local time, which is a split between the two. Over the river in Juarez they use Mexican time. Visited a barber shop for a shave, then a restaurant for breakfast and got another shave; I was taxed one dollar and twenty cents for breakfast for two. We didn't return for dinner.

Those of our party who did not visit Juarez last evening attended the State Firemen's ball and banquet under the escort of Colonel Whitmore, Acting Mayor of El Paso, and Chief J. J. Connors, of the city fire department, and they all speak in the highest terms of the royal treatment they received and the grand time they had. The city of El Paso contains about 12,000 inhabitants, but the population is almost double that number this week, which gives the town a very lively appearance. We learn that our train cannot be gotten over the washout to-day, and arrangements are being made to remain in the city to-night. Engaged a pleasant room for fifty cents per day at the "Wellington," corner of Staunton and Texas Streets, kept by Mrs. Whitmore; quite a number of our party are stopping here.

Brother Wyman hired a horse to-day and rode in the parade. It is very hot in the sun. Went over in front of the Court House this afternoon to see the firemen race. There was quite an exciting time. Brother Haas was there with his kodak and had a narrow escape from being run over in trying to get a "snap" at a team as the horses galloped past. Had a pleasant chat in the evening with Mr. Pettus, an old resident of the place, who has a furnishing store next to the "Wellington." He is an entertaining man and gave some interesting information relative to the early history and habits of the country and people. I turned in about eleven o'clock, but can't speak for them all, for this is an interesting city.

### FRIDAY, MAY 14th.

Turn out this morning about 7.30 and find the weather clear and warm. We go to a nearby restaurant for breakfast; mutton chops are one of the items on the bill of fare, and we are pleased, for we are partial to chops—nice, juicy, tender mutton chops; but these chops do not quite come up to our idea of what mutton chops should be—not so juicy nor so tender as we would like; but being hungry we quietly and uncomplainingly devour what is set before us. "Where do you people in El Paso get your mutton?" I inquired of the waiter as we arose from the table (for I had no recollection of seeing a sheep since we entered the State of Texas). *"Goats,"* was the short but suggestive answer. A little private inquiry elicited the information that it is a fact that the greater part of the "mutton" consumed in El Paso is a product of the goatherd. The supply is apparently inexhaustible, for thousands of those ruminating, odoriferous quadrupeds can be seen roaming the adjacent plains and plateaus in great herds, attended by boys and dogs.

Accompanied Manager Wyman to Superintendent Martin's office, where we learn "that there is no prospect of getting our train across the washout this week. The water has fallen but very little, and while we are working day and night, endeavoring to close the break, our progress is necessarily slow on account of the action of the high water, and the work cannot be completed sufficiently to get our train across until the water recedes. And no one knows," continued Mr. Martin, "when this will be, for the water is just as likely to rise as to fall. The weather has been very hot these last few days and has melted the snow in the mountains very rapidly, which has caused the high water here. When the snow is gone the water will fall, so you see it depends upon the supply of snow, of which we know nothing about. If you wish to continue on your journey I will send you to Los Angeles by regular train, and when we succeed in getting your train across will send it on after you."

Brother Wyman rather favors this proposition, as he desires to reach Los Angeles before the Grand Division adjourns, but the majority of our party will not agree to it, preferring to remain with the train and take their chance with it; so the idea of going ahead by regular train is abandoned. A party of us procured a four-horse team and went over to the train to-day, some to remain and others to return. Would have remained had Mrs. S. been along, for it is a dreadful hot trip of two and one-half hours across that burning sand.

We found our train sidetracked at Alfalfa, one mile east of the washout, and had one mile to walk after leaving the wagon. Alfalfa is not a place—it is only a name. There is a sidetrack here and a post with a board on it, and on the board is painted in large black letters the word ALFALFA. That is all. It is a flag-stop for accommodation trains, but there is no station, not even a shed, a platform, nor a plank. The nearest civilized communities are El Paso, 7 miles away to the west, and Fort Bliss, the same distance to the north. On the east end of the same sidetrack where our train lies are a number of cabooses of the Texas and Pacific construction train, occupied by Mexican families whose husbands and fathers are working on the repairs at the washout. They are a squalid, uninviting-looking set, but seem happy and contented with their lot.

Here and there in the edge of a sandbank can be seen a "dugout," or, sheltered in a mesquite thicket, a "shack" occupied by the same nationality, who with their goats and burros are very pictures of meek and lowly contentment. These are the surroundings in the midst of which we are sidetracked. We find our people (those who are with the train) with smiles upon their faces as they tell us they are "all right" and are having a good and pleasant time. There must surely be an element or ingredient in this desert air and atmosphere that breeds contentment and repose.

Several of the boys went over to the train and back on broncos to-day, and experienced a hot but exhilarating ride. The party consisted of Brothers Waddington, Taylor, Matthews, Moore, Mattson, Leary, and Elder, who all claim that the ride, although a very hot one, was rare sport. The novel experience of a ride of 14 miles on a fiery, wiry Texan horse is a feature of their visit to El Paso that will not be forgotten.

Brother Wyman remained at Alfalfa to watch the progress of repairs at the washout, and I returned in the wagon to El Paso. Dining-car Conductor McDonald accompanied us; he was looking for a wagonload of supplies for his car from El Paso that had not arrived. When about half way across the plateau we met the team. Mr. McDonald interviewed the driver to ascertain if his wagon was loaded with what had been ordered and found everything satisfactory.

As we leave behind us the hot, suffocating desert trail we pass close to the base of Mt. Franklin, in the shadow-of which El Paso lies, and crossing the railroad tracks of the Fort Bliss Branch we feel a deep sense of relief as we strike the hard, smooth street that leads us into the city's welcome shade and rest.

Learning on our arrival back that the El Paso *Telegraph*, a morning paper, contained an account of our scorching desert plateau. The party consists of nine, including the driver, in a large transfer coach drawn by two horses. To relieve the overburdened animals, the men walk part of the way and keep a sharp lookout for rattlesnakes, for the driver had hinted that we might encounter some, as they are known to be quite numerous in this locality. Two large snakes of an unknown species were seen; one glided into a hole in the side of the bank of a deep arroyo, and we did not go to look for him; the other was discovered lying quietly behind a large sage bush by one of the "boys," who silently imparted the information to the rest.

We gathered around, and looking where he pointed, saw a portion of his snakeship's form through a small opening in the bush. "Think it would be safe to shoot at him?" whispered the discoverer of the snake, as he clutched his ever-ready revolver in his grasp. "Yes; blaze away," answered a chorus of low voices. *Bang!* went the pistol, and we saw the snake slightly move, but it did not run away. "I hit him," exclaimed our brother with the pistol; and we all moved cautiously around the bush to investigate. There he was, sure enough, a greenish-striped fellow about six feet long, but he had no head, and from his appearance it had been three or four days since he had lost it. Our marksman's ball had struck the ground just underneath the body and turned it partly over, which movement had deceived us. I will say no *more* about it lest you guess who did the shooting; not that I think he would care, for mistakes are being made every day by some of us that are worse than shooting dead snakes.

Arriving at our train about noon, after an absence

FLOODED DISTRICT, ALFALFA, TEXAS.

WRECKED BY TRAIN ROBBERS ON SOUTHERN PACIFIC RAILWAY.

of three days, brings with it a feeling of relief, similar to getting home again. The majority of the party had preceded us, a number having come over yesterday. All express themselves as being glad to get back to the train, notwithstanding its uninviting surroundings and isolated condition. What we all appreciate very much and what goes far toward breaking the monotony of the situation is the fact that nearly all the Texas and Pacific and Southern Pacific trains stop here, and are very kind in furnishing us with water and ice when we need it.

Yesterday afternoon a Southern Pacific train stopped here that had been held up by train robbers a few miles east of Sierra Blanca. The safe in the express car was blown open with dynamite and robbed of a large amount of money. The train was held for one and a half hours while the work was being done. The passengers on the train were not molested. Some of our party entered the car and examined the wrecked safe, which was blown almost into fragments. A portion of the car roof was torn off by the force of the explosion and pieces of the safe were found in the sides and ends of the car. A parrot and a rooster in the car lost nearly all their feathers, but otherwise were apparently uninjured. Several of our party obtained parrot and rooster feathers and pieces of the safe as souvenirs. The Texan Rangers, we are told, are hot on the trail of the outlaws.

Manager Wyman has just returned from the washout and brings no encouragement. "The break cannot be repaired until the water falls two feet," says Brother Wyman, "and it shows no disposition to fall." "Give me two hundred men and the material to bridge those arroyos and lay the track and I will have a railroad from here into El Paso across that desert plateau inside the time they have been waiting for this water to fall," exclaimed Brother Sloane, spiritedly. "They won't leave you do it, Charlie," said Brother Terry, sympathetically. The arrival of six more of our people from El Paso and the announcement of dinner at the same time prevented further conversation in this direction.

We were favored with a light shower in the afternoon, which evidently stirred up the mosquitoes, for they are very numerous and aggressive this evening. This is a beautiful night. It is the full of the moon, and the clear, marvelous light it sheds is the most wonderful moonlight we have ever seen; so clear, so bright, and yet so soft; no one can describe it, for it is simply indescribable. Objects can be discerned at a remarkable distance, and Mt. Franklin, six miles away, looms up to the vision dark, grim, and majestic.

As our party one by one retire to their berths there is not a mind among them all but what is impressed with the beauty and grandeur of the night, the silence and serenity of which is broken only by the occasional barking of a watchful Mexican dog or the quarrelsome snarling of thieving coyotes.

## SUNDAY, MAY 16th.

To-day is clear and warm, with a delightful breeze stirring. We avoid the hot glare of the sun by remaining as much as possible on the shady side of the train. There are remarkable conditions of climate here. In the sun the heat is distressing, almost unbearable; in the shade it is more than comfortable, almost luxurious, producing a feeling of exuberant pleasure and vitality that is difficult to express or understand. There was a light thunder shower during the night, which no doubt had a tendency to further clarify and rarify this wonderful atmosphere. We are making the best of the situation; have plenty to eat and drink, but there is a scarcity of water for washing purposes, although large irrigating ditches are close to hand, but the waters are too muddy for use.

About noon a Southern Pacific work train came along and supplied our cars with water, which is hauled in large wooden tanks holding about 4000 gallons each. It is brought from Lasca, about 70 miles east of Alfalfa. S. P. engine No. 904 is drawing the train which is supplying us with water, Engineer John Condon, Conductor G. M. Seamonds, Brakemen J. M. Bates and Charles McDonald, who are very kind and obliging, carefully supplying each car with all the water needed. Manager Wyman has just received a telegram from Superintendent Martin saying that the break situation is not improving, and suggests that our committee make arrangements to go some other way.

Brakeman Charles Gunning, who has been with us since we left Ft. Worth, made suggestions to our committee which were immediately taken up, viz., that we return to Sierra Blanca and from there take the Southern Pacific to Spofford Junction, thence over Eagle Pass and the Mexican International to Torreon, then up over the Mexican Central to El Paso, making a triangle trip of about 1450 miles. The committee immediately set out to communicate with the railroad officials, and we are all waiting anxiously to know the result of the conference.

In the meantime work at the washout must have progressed with remarkable rapidity, for some one just from there brings the highly encouraging report that the break in the track is trestled over and the prospect of getting us away soon is good. This report comes less than three hours after Manager Wyman had received a message from Superintendent Martin saying "he could give us no hope; that we had better go some other way." Is it any wonder that we are doubtful of the good news and regard it as a fake? But it is true, nevertheless, for Brothers Wyman and Maxwell have just returned and verify the report, adding "that if the water does not rise again we will go out of here to-morrow."

Brothers Wyman, Maxwell, Sheppard, Gilliland, and myself walked down to the washout this evening and came back in the caboose of the work train. It is about three miles from where our train lies to the break in the track that has caused so much labor and anxiety. The greater part of this work is performed by Mexicans, and they have been working day and night, much of the time up to the waist in water, in order to get the break repaired. More of our party came over from El Paso this evening; they are all over now but two or three. Brothers Haas and Smith and Mrs. Smith went over to El Paso to-day to go by regular train to Los Angeles.

When Brother John Reilly came over to the train he brought with him a very much corroded revolver, presented as a souvenir to the Pennsylvania Railroad conductors' excursion party by Col. Si Ryan. The revolver belonged to George Daley, mining engineer, of Lake

WILLIAM J. MAXWELL, OF THE COMMITTEE.

Valley, New Mexico, who was killed by Indians September 9th, 1878. The revolver was found on the alkali plains where Engineer Daley met his death. The alkali had eaten off all the woodwork and corroded with rust the iron. It is an interesting relic and highly valued as a souvenir.

The "boys" have been patrolling the train at night since we have been sidetracked here. I have volunteered to go on second watch to-night, and turned in at eleven o'clock, expecting to be called at 2 A. M. for patrol duty.

## MONDAY, MAY 17th.

Awakened at 2.30 this morning by Brother George Dale, and with Brother Sam Horner go on duty to watch and to wait for morning to come. There is nothing else for us to do; all is quiet outside and around the train as we promenade back and forth on the alert for anything of a suspicious nature. The morning is clear and bright and the air cool and refreshing. Brother Kilgore, who sleeps near the roof in the car "Milton," is doing some vigorous snoring, and Brother Houston, in the rear of the "Orchis," is talking earnestly in his sleep. We catch an occasional glimpse of a skulking dog or coyote seeking for food amongst the scraps thrown from the train, but no marauder appears to molest us. A heavy 44-caliber six-shooter, presented to the writer just before starting on the trip by Lyttleton Johnson, Esq., of Chadd's Ford, Pa., has been at the service of our watchmen, and we feel that we are well armed. When not in possession of the watchmen, Baggagemaster George Anderson sleeps with it under his pillow.

The coming of day and the stir of the occupants of the cars relieve us from duty, and we strike out through the mesquite thicket to reconnoitre and obtain a view of our surroundings. Less than 200 yards from the train we come to a deep, wide, irrigating canal, through which the muddy water is rushing in a torrent. We can go no further in this direction and conclude to follow the stream in quest of a bridge. We go but a short distance when the thicket becomes impenetrable, and we retreat, and cutting a cane from the thicket as a memento of our little walk, we return to the train, glad to find that breakfast is ready and to learn that an effort will be made to get us over the break to-day.

Brother Wyman has been closely watching the progress of the repairs, and under the supervision of Master Mechanic H. Small, the work these last two days has made very rapid advancement. The sun is scorching hot and the forenoon is spent by the party sitting in groups in the shadow of the train discussing the various features of the situation, and many are the surmises as to what will be the result of an attempt to cross that sea of water over the repaired and trestled tracks with a train of cars of such weight as ours. We feel that the risk is great, but realize the effort to get us over is to be made, when about 1 P. M. S. P. engine No. 719, in charge of Engineer M. Love, is run in against our train and we are pushed, with six construction cars ahead of us, out on the main track and up toward the flooded district. Conductor J. H. Ludwig has charge of the train, and in him Mrs. Ed. Foster recognizes a cousin whom she had not seen for many years. The recognition is mutual and the meeting a happy one. The knowledge that the conductor is related to and personally known by a member of our party creates a feeling of confidence that almost assures our safe deliverance.

We have now reached high water and our train is being slowly pushed farther and farther into a gurgling, surging, muddy flood until the dreaded break is reached, with miles of water all around us. The repaired track, propped and trestled, settles and sinks out of sight when it receives the weight of the cars, that toss and roll and creak in a manner which, if it does not frighten us, fills us with much concern, for we are afraid we will lose our train in the flood. A sudden stop, caused by the bursting of an air-brake hose on the engine, fills us with alarm. "We are lost," murmured Mrs. Maxwell, and her face wore a frightened look. "Not yet," replied Brother Schuler, and his assurance gave us comfort; but the few minutes delay caused by the accident was almost fatal, for our heavy dining car had settled until its wheels were covered with water and the repairsmen thought a rail had broken beneath its weight. In water almost up to their necks the men made an examination of the track under the car and found it intact.

The signal was given to move ahead, and as slowly the sunken car comes into position, hearts become lighter and faces grow brighter; the dreadful suspense is over, and we give more attention to our surroundings. We see many fine residences surrounded by water, and large fields of grain inundated and ruined. We are two hours coming through the four miles of high water. Slowly and carefully we are safely brought through, and all concerned are entitled to the highest praise for the able and judicious manner in which the train was handled.

Arriving at the Southern Pacific station in El Paso about three o'clock, and finding we have an hour before leaving, many avail themselves of the opportunity of taking a parting look at this interesting city and bidding adieu to the many kind friends who have done so much toward making our forced stay a pleasant and happy one. Four of our party, under the escort of Brother Sloane, have taken a trip over to Juarez, and much uneasiness and concern is felt for them, as the time is up for our train to go and they have not returned. The engine whistle is sounded long and loud to call them in, but they do not come. "They have gone over there to make some purchases," asserts Brother Sheppard, "and I fear have been arrested for trying to evade the customs laws." "No fear of that," replies Captain Purcell, who has charge of our train, "you may rest assured that no member of your party will be molested by the customs officers. The courtesy and freedom of the cities of El Paso and Juarez have been extended to you, and the badge you wear is a guarantee of your safety." "Yes," adds Col. Si Ryan, who is on hand to see us off, "Diaz wouldn't allow any of you Pennsylvanians pinched if you should carry off the whole State of Chihuahua, for his Honor thinks Pennsylvania the greatest and best State of the Union, with the exception, of course, of Texas," and there is a proud, faraway look in the Colonel's eye as he contemplates the enormous area and the illimitable possibilities of the great Lone Star State. Notwithstanding the assurance of Captain Purcell and Colonel Ryan, Brother Post is very much concerned, for Miss Ella is with the absent party, and he has gone to look for them. Brothers Moore and Dougherty have

COL. S[?] RYAN.

taken advantage of the delay and are off looking for souvenirs. Those who are waiting for the return of the absent ones are growing very impatient, and when at last they are seen coming, impatience and uneasiness give way to feelings of relief and gladness, and Brother Sloane is forgiven once more on the plea "that it was a misunderstanding of the time that caused the trouble," and gave it as his opinion that "El Paso time is one of the most confusing problems that ever worried a tourist."

The deep-toned engine bell peals out the warning that the train is about to start; "All aboard" is shouted, the last hand shake is given, and at 5.45 (2.45 Pacific) P. M., just five days, six hours, and forty-five minutes late, our train rolled out of the Southern Pacific Station and across the Rio Grande, leaving behind the pretty and interesting city of El Paso and our many new-found friends, whose liberality and kindness will ever remain a pleasant and happy memory with us. Our train is drawn by S. P. engine No. 1395, in charge of Engineer Joseph Bird and fired by J. V. Paul, who accompany us to Tucson, 312 miles. Conductor T. H. Purcell and Brakeman E. G. Shaub go with us to Yuma, 563 miles.

We are in New Mexico, having entered it when we crossed the Rio Grande River. The country is wild and barren and the railroad very crooked. Engineer Bird, in his eagerness to make up the lost time, is running at a speed which Manager Wyman thinks is not consistent with safety. The cars rock and roll in an alarming manner, and several dishes have been broken in the dining car, which calls forth a protest from our friend McDonald of that most cherished department. Brother Wyman immediately requests Conductor Purcell to instruct the engineer to reduce speed, which is done, much to the relief and comfort of all on board. Brother Joseph Flory, of St. Louis Division No. 3, State Railroad and Warehouse Commissioner, of Jefferson City, Mo., and Harry Steere, Esq., traveling passenger agent of the Southern Pacific Railroad, are our guests from El Paso to Los Angeles, and a much appreciated acquisition to our party.

They have a fund of useful and interesting information on hand pertaining to the country through which we are passing, which they impart to us in a pleasant and entertaining manner. "What place is this, Mr. Steere?" we inquire as a pretty little town bursts upon our vision. "This is Deeming," replies Mr. Steere, "and it is quite an important place. We are now 88 miles from El Paso, and this is the first town we have seen. A few years ago it was as barren and uninhabitable here as any of the desolate country through which we have passed, but good water was discovered a few feet below the surface of the ground, and now the place is noted for its many wells of fine water, which is shipped for hundreds of miles and is also used for irrigating purposes, for nothing will grow throughout this region unless it is artificially watered. The thrifty young shade trees, the shrubbery and patches of verdant vegetation you noticed as we passed through Deeming is convincing evidence that all this region needs, to make it one of the most fertile and productive countries in the world, is plenty of water."

For 60 miles further we pass through this region of desert plateaus known as the plains of Deeming. The dust is almost suffocating and sifts through every crack and crevice, the double, almost air-tight, windows of the Pullmans being insufficiently close to keep it out. At the little station of Lordsburg, 60 miles from Deeming, Engineer Bird stops to water his iron horse. "This supply of water," remarked Mr. Steere, "is brought here in pipes from a large spring or lake in yonder mountain, five miles away."

Looking in the direction indicated, we can see through the gathering dusk of evening the dark outlines of a mountain in the distance. " 'Tis a pity," continued Mr. Steere, "that you were not enabled to pass through this section during daylight, for there are some things I should like you to see. We are drawing near the Arizona line, and the scenery is becoming more broken and varied. Those mountains which you can dimly discern on your right are composed of cliffs and crags of reddish rock of a peculiar and interesting formation. On the left the great San Simon Valley stretches away to the south for a distance of 75 or 80 miles, and is the grazing ground for many thousands of cattle. One company alone, the San Simon Cattle Company, it is said, has a herd of nearly 100,000 head." "What do they feed on, Mr. Steere?" I asked, for visions of the dust-environed plains of Deeming were still floating in my mind. "This great valley," answered Mr. Steere, "through the northern boundary of which we are now passing, is not nearly so dry as the more elevated country through which we have passed. There are occasionally short periods of wet weather which produces pasture very rapidly, the pasture consisting chiefly of what is known through here as gama grass, which grows very fast and luxuriant and possesses great feeding qualities. The strangest but most valuable feature of this peculiar vegetation is that it retains all its sweetness and nutrition after it is dead and brown, and stock feed upon it with as much avidity in a dry and sapless condition as they do when they find it in the green and juicy stage of life and growth.

"Away to the south, bounding this immense valley, is a wild and rocky range of the Chiricahua Mountains, said to be from time immemorial the rendezvous of renegades and desperadoes, one of the most noted being an outlaw Apache Indian called the 'Arizona Kid,' whose depredations and crimes were a terror to all the surrounding country. And were it only light," continued Mr. Steere, "I would show you one of the most notable landmarks on the Southern Pacific Road. Away over to the south there, clearly outlined against the sky, is a mountain formation that plainly resembles the upturned profile of a human face. It is called 'Cochise's Head,' bearing a strong likeness, it is said, to Cochise, the most noted chieftain of the Apache tribe."

We have now reached what is known as "Territorial Line," about midway between the little stations of Stein's Pass and San Simon. Conductor Purcell kindly stops the train at this point, giving those who wish the opportunity and privilege of gathering some mementoes of the occasion and locality. I look at my watch; it is 11.20 P. M. "Philadelphia" time, 8.20 P. M. "Territorial Line" time; it is pretty dark for the business on hand, but the post that marks the dividing line is easily found, and in a very short time is so badly cut and splintered by the relic hunters that it looks as though it had been struck by lightning. Several standing astride the designated and imaginary dividing line picked pebbles from New Mexico and Arizona at the same time. In five minutes we are on our way again, and in a short time thereafter the snores of the tourists heard above the rumble of the train proclaim that "the weary are at rest."

## TUESDAY, MAY 18th.

Got up this morning about the usual time and found that we had passed Tucson in the early part of the morning and had changed engines at that point. We have now S. P. engine No. 9030, Engineer J. W. Bunce and Fireman J. Weir, who run us to Yuma, a distance of 251 miles. It cannot always be day, nor we cannot always be awake, so when night comes and we sleep we miss much that is novel and interesting. "You have missed much since entering Arizona that is well worth seeing," I hear Mr. Steere remark to several of the party with whom he is conversing as I enter the smoker. "During the night we have passed through the most wonderful cactus country in the world, many of the plants rising to the height of thirty and forty feet; but you will see similar plants should you pass through the Antelope Valley, Cal., in daytime after leaving Los Angeles. You also missed seeing the town of Benson, which is one of the important places on this line, where we connect with the New Mexico and Arizona and the Arizona and Southwestern Railroads; and it is really too bad that you did not get at least a passing look at Tucson, for there is only one Tucson in the world. It is one of the oldest and queerest places

in the United States, and a place with a history. The
population is estimated to be about 8000, and nearly
all of the residences are of adobe construction. Claims
are made that it was first settled by the Spanish in
1560." A call to breakfast interrupted Mr. Steere's interesting talk as we all make a break for the dining car.

All the morning we have been descending the Gila
River Valley, and the picturesque, complex scenery of
mountain, plain, and valley has been much enjoyed by
all. As we approach Yuma, situated on the Colorado
River, in the extreme southwestern corner of Arizona,
we can scarcely realize that in the 251 miles we have
come since leaving Tucson we have dropped from an
altitude of 2390 feet to that of 140 feet, the elevation
of Yuma, but such is the case, according to the figures
given on the time table of the Southern Pacific Railroad
which I hold in my hand, and which Captain Purcell
and Mr. Steere both declare is correct beyond a shadow
of doubt, adding "that the Southern Pacific Railroad
Company was never known to publish a falsehood or
make a mistake."

We arrive at Yuma 12.30 P. M. Eastern (9.30 A. M.
Pacific), and make a stop of fifteen minutes. The station is a low-built, commodious building, surrounded
on three sides by extensive grounds in which flowers
are blooming in profusion. A number of bouquets
were gathered by the ladies. Several native Indians
are about the station having for sale trinkets and toys
of their own manufacture. It is a strange and novel
sight to behold these old remnants of an almost extinct race and tribe dressed in the scant and grotesque
garb of their nativity, with their faces and the exposed

ARIZONA LANDSCAPE.

"YUMA BILL," INDIAN CHIEF AT YUMA, OVER 100 YEARS OLD.

parts of their limbs and bodies painted and tattooed with bright and varied colors, increasing tenfold their natural ugliness, which showing to its best advantage, unassisted by art, is far above par. Yuma Bill, the biggest, oldest, and ugliest of the lot, seems to claim the most attention, and as I see him coming down the station platform and entering the waiting-room door, bareheaded and barefooted, with a bright-striped blanket about him, I think of Mark Twain's story of his visit to the camp of Sitting Bull. "The old chief saw me coming," says Mark, "and he came to meet me. I had pictured him in my mind as an old warrior covered with glory; I found him clothed with the nobility of his race, assisted by an old horse blanket, one corner of which hid his approach and the other corner covered his retreat." Similar characters are Yuma Bill and his pals, and if ever "Mark" encounters them he will be strongly reminded of his notable interview with the famous Sitting Bull.

We all buy trinkets of Bill, for we never expect to see him again and we don't want to forget him. We are told that he is a good old Indian, but was not always so. Years ago, when there were battles to be won, Bill made a record as a fighter. He will fight no more; there are only a few of him left; and Uncle Sam has given him and his comrades a refuge in a little reservation across the river where they hope to live and die in quietness and peace.

A short distance back of the station can be seen the territorial prison or penitentiary, on a bluff overlooking the Colorado River. We thought it was a fort until told that it was a prison. Our train is about to start, and we find a large car or tank of water attached on the front end next the engine and a freight caboose on the rear. We find that a freight crew has charge of us, that the tank of water will be needed to supply the engine, as there is a run of 120 miles through a country devoid of water, and that the crew will need the caboose when they leave us, for they expect to take back from Indio a train of freight. We have S. P. engine No. 1609, with Engineer W. Hayes at the throttle, fired by George McIntyre, Conductor H. J. Williams, Brakemen H. J. Schulte and R. M. Armour. As our train moves slowly off across the bridge that spans the Colorado we take a last look at Yuma and its picturesque surroundings, and in two minutes we are in California and crossing the Colorado Desert.

We are disappointed. We thought California a land of beauty, fertility, and flowers—a desert waste is all we see, bald mountains and barren plains on every side. Our course is upward for about 25 miles, until an elevation of 400 feet is reached, and then we begin to descend, and when we pass the little station of Flowing Well, 60 miles west of Yuma, we are only five feet above the level of the sea. Ten miles farther we stop at Volcano Springs and are 225 feet below the sea level. After leaving Flowing Well our attention was called by Mr. Steere to what was apparently a large lake of clear, sparkling water ahead, and to the left of our train, about half a mile away. We were running toward it but got no closer to it. It remained there, the same distance from us, a bright, sparkling, rippling body of water; not one on the train but what would have said, "It is water." Mr. Steere says, "No; it is not water;

THE CALIFORNIA POPPY.

it is a delusion, a mirage caused by the glare of the sun on the shining salt crust of this alkali desert. There is not much doubt," continued Mr. Steere, "but what ages upon ages ago all this immense basin was the bottom of a great sea. You can see upon the sides of these barren bluffs and upon those walls of rock the mark of the water line that for thousands of years perhaps have withstood the ravages and test of time. This little station is called Volcano Springs because of the number of springs in this locality that are apparently of volcanic origin. They are not in operation at the present time, but certain seasons of the year they are very active and spout up mud and water to a height of from 10 to 25 feet."

A thermometer hanging in the doorway of the station, in the shade, registers 101 degrees, and it is not unusual, we are told, for it to reach 125. It is actually too hot in the sun to stand still; it almost takes one's breath away. We feel relieved when our train starts and we are in motion once more. We create a breeze, a sea breeze, as it were, wafted to us o'er the mummified saliniferous remains of an ancient sea 3000 years a corpse. But the "mirage" still is there, a wonderful delusion, a monstrous deception, a gigantic "Will o' the wisp," whose alluring promises have led hundreds of men and animals a fruitless chase that ended in horrid death.

Sixty-five miles ahead of us we can plainly see San Jacinto Mountain, towering 11,500 feet in the air, with its summit covered with ice and snow that glistens in the noonday sun. Twenty-four miles from Volcano Springs we pass Salton, noted for its great salt industry. This is the lowest point on the line of the Southern Pacific

Railroad, being 263 feet below sea level. About three miles to the left of the railroad we see the great white salt marsh or lake, containing such a vast deposit of this useful substance that the supply is thought to be inexhaustible. Steam plows are used for gathering the salt, and the works erected here have a capacity of nearly 1000 tons per day.

Twenty-five miles from Salton we reach Indio, where a short stop is made to change engines. Indio is a veritable oasis in the desert. After miles and miles of desert dust and glaring sand, it is very refreshing to see again trees and grass and flowers. We are still 20 feet below the level of the sea, but good water has been found here, and plenty of it applied to the soil has worked wonders. Whatever is planted grows with rapidity and in profusion, and with an abundance of water Indio can look forward to fast increasing beauty and prosperity. It has been discovered that the climate here is very beneficial to consumptives, and Indio has already become noted as a resort for those afflicted with pulmonary trouble, and it is claimed some very remarkable cures have been effected.

We leave Indio at 4.15 P. M. Eastern (1.15 P. M. Pacific), with S. P. engine No. 1397. Engineer Ward Heins, Fireman J. A. Shanehan; Conductor Williams and his brakemen will continue on to Los Angeles with us, 130 miles further.

Soon after leaving Indio we ascend a grade of 120 feet to the mile and pass along the base of San Jacinto Mountain, with its summit frowning down upon us from a height of 11,500 feet. The snow can now be plainly seen upon its highest peaks, and rivulets and cataracts can be seen in places dashing and leaping down its seamed and rugged sides.

At Rimlon we get Engineer Eli Steavens and Fireman M. Anderson with engine No. 1963 to assist us up a steep grade to Beaumont, a distance of 35 miles.

At Palm Springs a short stop was made to take aboard some guests who came to meet us from Los Angeles. They were Mr. G. L. Mead, Mr. H. Kearney, and Mr. J. E. White. Mr. Mead is a merchant of Los Angeles who heard of our coming and came to meet us to bid us welcome to the "Paradise of America," and to emphasize his expressions of good feelings, presented the tourists with a case of very fine California wine. Mr. Mead could have done nothing more in accord with the feelings of the party. No wine ever tasted better, no wine ever did more good; it is a medicine our systems crave after 150 miles of the scorching, glaring, waterless Colorado Desert; a right thing in the right place; it is appreciated far more than Mr. Mead will ever know. Mr. Kearney is a promoter of stage lines and is about to establish a route between Palm Springs and Virginia Dale, a distance of 71 miles. He is an interesting gentleman to converse with, being perfectly familiar with all the surrounding country. Mr. White is a transfer agent doing business in Los Angeles, and is on hand to render aid to any of the party who may need his services.

We arrive at Beaumont and have reached the summit of the grade. In the 50 miles we have come since leaving Indio, we have made an ascent of 5280 feet. Our helper engine No. 1397 has left us, and we commence our descent of the western slope of the San Bernardino

Range. Mr. J. Jacobs, a civil engineer in the employ of the Southern Pacific Railroad Company, was invited to get aboard at Beaumont and accompany us to Los Angeles. We find him a very agreeable guest, giving us a great deal of entertaining information.

We have passed from desert wastes into a rich agricultural district; farmers are engaged in harvesting hundreds of acres of barley, which in this region is cut while in a green state and cured for hay. We pass many large fruit orchards of different varieties, while away in the distance on every hand the mountains rear their snow-clad peaks to the clouds. It is a grand and wonderful transformation from the scenes through which we have lately passed, and needs to be seen to be appreciated.

"This section of country through which we are now passing," observed Mr. Jacobs, "is the famous Redlands district, a country that has shown far greater development and been subject to more rapid improvements in the same number of years than any other known section of its size in the world. Ten years ago it was almost barren, and known only as a vast sheep range; to-day, owing to a thorough system of irrigation, there are nearly 30,000 acres of reclaimed land that bloom and blossom and bear fruit with all the fertility, the beauty, and abundance of a tropical garden."

We have now entered the orange district, and large groves are seen on every hand, golden with the luscious fruit. At Pomona a halt of sufficient length is made to allow several baskets of oranges to be put on the train, which are distributed amongst the party and found to be delicious and refreshing. We are unable to ascertain who are the thoughtful donors, but all the

A CLUSTER OF NAVEL ORANGES, CALIFORNIA.

same they have the most sincere thanks of the entire party for their kindness and generosity.

For 25 miles we pass through a fairyland of blooming loveliness, and at 8.45 P. M. Eastern (5.45 Pacific) our train rolls into the station in Los Angeles, five days, five hours, and forty-five minutes late. On an adjacent track a train is loading, and we learn it is the New York Central excursion about ready to start for home. We exchange greetings and cards with many of them before their train pulls out, bound for its journey through the heat and dust of desert and plain, for they return by the route we came, and we know what is in store for them.

We begin to realize what we have missed by thus coming in at the eleventh hour. We find we were saved from a watery grave in the raging Rio Grande only to discover that we are here just in time to be too late to participate in the "good times" all the other visitors have had. The twenty-sixth session of the Grand Division of the "Order of Railway Conductors" that we had expected to attend is about ready to adjourn; the pleasure trips planned for the entertainment of members of the order to all the surrounding points of interest have been taken, and we weren't "in it." 'Tis rather a discouraging outlook, but with the true Yankee spirit of self-reliance we quickly determine to make the best of it, trusting our future to luck and Providence.

Brothers Houston, Haefner, and myself start for Music Hall, No. 234 South Spring Street, where the Convention is in session, and arrive five minutes before its adjournment. We hear Brother Grand Chief Conductor E. E. Clark make his closing speech. As the members of the Convention commence to pour out of the hall into the street the greater part of our folks arrive on the scene, and for more than an hour an impromptu meeting is held on the sidewalk and on the street in front of the building, where old friends are greeted and new friends are made; everybody wants to exchange cards with everybody else; all are good-natured, good-humored, and happy, and "perpetual friendship" seems to be the ruling spirit of the hour. The crowd gradually disperses and becomes scattered over the city, members of our party mingling with the rest, seeing the sights and looking for souvenirs.

Brother Ristein received a telegram that had been lying in the Los Angeles office four days awaiting his arrival, telling him of the serious illness of one of his children far away in his Delmar home, and he is at the office now, anxiously awaiting a reply to a message of inquiry sent as to the present condition of the child. Brother Ristein fears the worst, and we all share his anxiety. Promptly the answer flashes back, "The child is better and thought to be out of danger." The words make light a heavy heart, and we are all glad for Brother Ristein's sake.

Our train occupies a track in the Arcade Station train shed for our convenience, and by ten o'clock there are very few but what have turned in. A few of the "boys" are still out, of course, but it is a hopeless task to try and "keep tab" on them. We cannot do it. These nocturnal outings of theirs will have to be noted down as "unwritten history." How much of it there will be we cannot tell. There has been considerable already, of which we might mention one night at Fort

WINTER IN SOUTHERN CALIFORNIA.

Worth, testing the efficacy of police protection while attempting to follow a "blind trail"; four or five nights in El Paso chasing the fleeting phantom of merry luck to the musical whirl of the wheel of fortune. They are all right, these "boys" of ours, and they know a good thing when they see it.

## WEDNESDAY, MAY 19th.

We are all up bright and early this morning, and after breakfast parties are formed to take in the sights. A number of us have decided to take a tally-ho ride, and Brother Wyman has gone to procure the outfit. In a short time he returns with the information that "the wagon will soon be here." It is not long until a fine roomy coach, drawn by six white horses, reins up in front of the group, and we clamber in. There is just room enough. We count the party and find there are fourteen, including the driver. The team is from the Panorama Stables and driven by "Mac," the veteran stager and coachman, who knows every crook and turn in all the highways and byways and drives and trails throughout Southern California. "Mac" is a character; we try to draw him out, but he won't talk about himself, won't even tell you his name, only that it is "Mac." He will tell you about everything else, and he is thoroughly posted. He takes us through the principal streets of this most wonderful city, rightly named "The town of the Queen of Angels."

Los Angeles lies amongst the foothills of the Sierra Madre Mountains, with an average elevation of 300 feet above sea level, only 15 miles from the coast, with an active, bustling business population of about 75,000 inhabitants. The beauty and magnificence of this tropical profusion through which we are passing is something we have heard of, but never saw before, and we find we are helpless when we attempt to describe it. In fancy and in dreams we have pictured "The Land of Sunshine and Flowers," but now, brought face to face with this marvelous reality, the beautiful pictures of dreams and fancy pale into crudeness and insignificance. Through avenues shaded on either side by rows of palms, eucalyptus, and pepper trees, past rose-embowered cottages and lawns filled with tropical plants, surrounded by hedges of roses and calla lilies, we continue on our way out through the suburbs into the rural districts, through the avenues of vast orange groves, the trees loaded with luscious golden fruit, through beautiful Pasadena, and on until "Mac" draws up at the famous ostrich farm, where we alight and go in to look around.

We spend about half an hour looking at the birds and two and a half dollars in the purchase of feathers. Loading up, we start on our way again, bound for "Lucky Baldwin's" ranch, "the largest individual tract of land," says "Mac," "in Southern California. It comprises 50,000 acres, nearly all under a condition of cultivation and improvement." Here it is our pleasure to behold the largest and most wonderful orange grove in the world. For miles we see nothing but orange trees and oranges; the trees are loaded and the ground is covered with the yellow fruit. We feast upon the beauty and grandeur of this unusual sight, with lots of oranges thrown in. It is needless to state that we ate all we could and loaded up the hack.

BROOKSIDE AVENUE, REDLANDS, CALIFORNIA.

A few miles further on we arrive at the Bonita Hotel, belonging to the ranch kept by Mrs. Warner, where the horses are taken from the coach and fed and the party takes lunch. Large lawns surround the buildings filled with many varieties of flowers, and we are given the privilege of plucking all we want, and when we leave each lady carries a large bouquet in her hand and each gentleman a smaller one in his buttonhole.

Starting on our way again, the horses refreshed with rest and food, we speed along lengthy drives and avenues, shaded by large Lombardy poplar and eucalyptus trees, for about two miles, when we pass through a large gateway over which is an arch in the form of an immense horse shoe, and enter the stable grounds where Baldwin's famous blooded horses are kept. We are kindly received by the stableman, shown through the stalls, where a number of the celebrated equines are seen. Brother Layfield evinces such a surprising knowledge of horseflesh and shows so much interest in the history of the different animals as related by the stableman that he is presented by that courteous gentleman with a mule's shoe as a souvenir of the visit. Brother Kilgore is also interested in the horses and would like to have a shoe; a search for one is unsuccessful, and so long did Brother Kilgore remain in the stable looking for the much-desired relic that he came near being left.

Leaving the stable grounds, we drive a mile further to the palatial residence and magnificent grounds of the renowned ruler of these domains. Mr. Baldwin is not at home at the present time, but the place is in charge of trusted employes. Leaving the coach, we walk through the spacious grounds surrounding the princely mansion.

Paradise can hardly be more beautiful and grand—the largest, the sweetest, the reddest roses that ever delighted the sense of sight or smell, the grandest trees, the most beautiful shrubbery bearing flowers of every kind and color. Bordered with blooming lilies are lakes of water, clear as crystal, on the surface of which graceful swans are swimming and in whose depth gold and silver fish dart and dive. Fine fountains and statuary intersperse the lawn, adding to its richness and beauty. Mounted above a pedestal in a conspicuous spot we notice an old bell. It is possessed of no beauty, and we wonder what it is for. We inquire of an old man working near by, "Uncle, what is the old rusty bell for?" "That old bell," answered the old gentleman, removing his hat with a low bow as he turns toward the object in question, "is the most valued thing you see. It is a relic that money cannot buy. Mr. Baldwin prizes it very highly, and we people all adore it." As the old servant utters the last words he makes another low courtesy. We begin to think he is a little daft and are about to move on, when, straightening up and with outstretched arm he points toward the old bell a bony, trembling finger, and continues slowly and with emphasis, "That old bell came from the chimes tower of the San Gabriel Mission. That is why we prize it; that is why we love it." We thought at first the old fellow bowed to us; we know now that he bowed to the old bell out of respect and reverence, for whatever is connected or associated with those old missions is looked upon as something almost sacred by many of the people here, especially those of the Roman faith.

A whistle from "Mac" informs us we must be going,

SAN GABRIEL MISSION, CALIFORNIA.

GIANT PALMS ON THE ROAD TO SAN GABRIEL.

and climbing into the 'bus the horses start off on a brisk trot and we soon leave "Lucky Baldwin's" ranch behind and enter "Sunny Slope" vineyard, owned by L. J. Rose. This immense vineyard contains 1500 acres and is traversed by beautiful avenues which divide this vast acreage of grapevines into great squares.

We are soon across this interesting tract and enter the grounds of the vintage plant of the San Gabriel Wine Company. We were very courteously treated and shown through the large establishment, the capacity of which is 1,500,000 gallons of wine per year. Upon leaving we pass through their vineyard, containing 1000 acres, which is near the vintage plant.

As we approach the old San Gabriel Mission and "Mac" reins up his steeds in front of the low, quaint building, I instinctively glance up at the ancient belfry and find that two of the niches or arches where bells once had swung are vacant. "Lucky Baldwin" has one of the bells; I wonder who has the other. At this moment another tally-ho drives up and stops, and we find it is a coaching party of our own people. We all alight and enter the historic and sacred edifice. Those who are of the faith render their acknowledgment with quiet, humble reverence; we who are not stand silently by in an attitude of mute veneration. San Gabriel stands fourth in the line of the twenty-one missions established in California from July 16th, 1769, to April 25th, 1820, the date of its establishment being September 8th, 1771.

The party we encountered consists of Mr. and Mrs. Mitchell, Mr. and Mrs. Maxwell, Mr. and Mrs. Reilly, Mr. and Mrs. Matthews, Mr. Reagan, Mr. McCarty, Mr. Waddington, Mr. Taylor, Mr. Williams, and Mr.

Suter. They occupy one of Hoag's White Livery tally-ho coaches, followed by Mr. and Mrs. Horner in a buggy. Our party consists of Mr. and Mrs. Wyman, Mr. and Mrs. Kilgore, Mr. and Mrs. Layfield, Mr. and Mrs. McKernan, Mr. and Miss Barrett, Mr. Crispen, Mrs. Shaw and myself.

As we bowl along the level drive toward the city, after leaving the old Mission, our conversation turns upon the pleasures of the day and of the interesting and beautiful things we have seen. We are all well pleased with our day's outing, especially the Colonel, who is in a high good humor, for had he not obtained what no one else could get, a substantial memento of his visit to the famous Baldwin ranch? "I am going to have this shoe decorated with ribbon and hung up in my parlor," asserts the Colonel, as he searches in the bottom of the coach for his prize. "I guess not," exclaims Mrs. Shaw, as she gives him a dig in the ribs with her elbow, "that's my shoe you've got hold of." "But where's my horse shoe? Has any one got it? Has any one seen my horse shoe?" excitedly inquires the Colonel, as he makes another dive into the bottom of the coach. "I think it flew away," quietly remarks Mrs. Wyman, as she draws her feet up and out of the way. "Who ever saw a shoe fly," snaps the Colonel, as he continues rummaging in the bottom of the vehicle. "I have," answers Manager Wyman, removing his hat, exposing a pate as devoid of hair and as bald as a door knob, from which he brushes an imaginary fly. "I saw a horse fly, but didn't notice if he had shoes on," observes Mrs. McKernan, keeping her eye on the Colonel, who is growing desperate in his failure to find

AN AVENUE IN PASADENA, CALIFORNIA.

his treasure. But it was gone; it had escaped from the bottom of the coach in some way, and we all sympathize with Brother Layfield in his bereavement, now that we find he has actually lost his valued souvenir.

We enter the city through East Side Park, which is a most beautiful and delightful drive. We bid goodbye to "Mac" and his spanking team and hurry to our dining car, where we arrive just in time for one of McDonald's dandy dinners, which we heartily enjoy after such a busy day. We find a number of our party had taken trips similar to our own, and over nearly the same route; others had ascended Mt. Lowe, been away above the clouds; some had taken a run down to Santa Monica and sported in the surf of the Pacific; some to Santa Catalina Island, the alleged "Garden of Eden" of the Pacific coast. All express themselves as having had an exceedingly good time and are laying plans for the morrow. There are many places we would like to visit and many things we would like to see, but our time is too limited "to take it all in," for we are to leave here to-morrow at 2.00 P. M. We have friends in San Diego we had intended to visit and there are fish at Catalina Island we had expected to catch; both friends and fish will have to charge their disappointment or pleasure, as the case may be, to the turbid waters of the Rio Grande.

Dinner being over, the most of our people take a walk up town and enjoy a promenade through the brilliantly-lighted streets, admiring the handsomely-furnished stores, with goods and wares arranged and exposed in so tempting a manner that many trinkets and knicknacks are purchased for souvenirs. Returning to the train at an early hour and hearing such a favorable account of the trip to Mt. Lowe from some who were there to-day, we conclude to join a party that is going in the morning and "take it in." One by one and two by two our people keep dropping in like unto the oft-mentioned fowls that "come home to roost," until only a few of the "boys," as usual, are left outside the fold, and to them I need again ascribe *"unwritten history."* As I leave the smoker to retire to my berth in the "Marco" I see our faithful George H. (Alfalfa) Anderson making up his bed, under the pillow of which he carefully places our "artillery," and I feel we are as safe as though surrounded by a cordon of Gatling guns.

### THURSDAY, MAY 20th.

Arose early this morning and found the weather not very favorable for our contemplated trip to Mt. Lowe, being cloudy and somewhat foggy, but we concluded to go, so after breakfast the party, consisting of Mr. and Mrs. Wyman, Mr. and Mrs. Layfield, Mr. and Miss Barrett, Mr. Kilgore, Mr. Sloane, Mr. Haas, Mr. Crispen, Mr. Denniston, two guests—Miss R. Stradling and Mr. A. L. Bailey—George H. Alfalfa Anderson, and myself, under the escort of Brother Ed. Butcher, of Los Angeles Division No. 111, who is a passenger conductor on the Los Angeles Terminal Road, boarded a car at 10.00 A. M. Eastern (7.00 A. M. Pacific) on the Pasadena and Los Angeles Electric Railway, conducted by W. A. Brown, and started on a never-to-be-forgotten trip to Mt. Lowe.

Out through the suburbs of Los Angeles, with its

GREAT CABLE INCLINE, MT. LOWE RAILWAY.

beautiful rose-embowered cottages and palatial residences and lawns of palms and tropical shrubbery, on through miles of country districts, rich with groves of golden fruit, through eden—Pasadena to Altadena, where we change cars for another electric road that carries us for about three miles over hill and dale, through ravines and across frightful-looking chasms, but always tending upward, until at an elevation of 2200 feet Rubio Cañon is reached and we are at the foot of the great cable incline, claimed to be the most wonderful cable road in the world, extending from Rubio Pavilion to Echo Mountain, a distance of 3000 feet. It makes a direct ascent of 1350 feet. Looking up at the wonderful construction it seems to almost pierce the sky; its summit is enshrouded in a veil of fog that hides it from our view.

"I don't quite like the looks of that," ventures Brother Kilgore, looking over his glasses with a scrutinizing glance, as his eyes follow the great incline up to where it is lost in the fog. "I guess it's all right; I don't think we'll find it as terrifying as it looks to be; anyhow, the proof of the pudding is in eating it, and I for one am going up," answers Brother Sloane. "Charlie, if you go I will go," responds his bosom friend and chum, Brother Haas. "There is no danger I will not share with you, and perhaps we can see some mountain goats."

"Or capture a deer," adds Brother Denniston, who is keeping pretty close to Miss Stradling, for that young lady looks as though she needs sympathy and companionship in this trying ordeal.

"Do you think it's safe, Charlie?" quietly inquires

Mrs. Wyman of her husband as we start to ascend to the landing where we board the car. "Yes, perfectly safe," replies Manager Wyman. "Human skill and ingenuity can make it no safer. They claim they never had an accident since the road has been in operation. The cable by which these cars are drawn has been tested to stand a strain of 100 tons, and the cars when loaded do not weigh five tons, so there is no danger at all." "If I thought there was the least danger I wouldn't go up," utters Brother Layfield, "but I know there isn't a bit." Mrs. Layfield makes no comment, but clings nervously to the Colonel's arm. The rest of the party follow without any apparent trepidation with the exception of "Alfalfa," who looks a trifle pale.

We are all comfortably seated in the "White Chariot" car, which is constructed without canopy or covering, with seats arranged in amphitheatre style, one above the other, facing the foot of the incline, an excellent arrangement for affording an unobstructed view.

The signal is given, the machinery is set in motion, and quietly and smoothly we start on our trip toward the sky.

"Those mountain peaks you see just beyond Rubio Cañon are called the 'Rubio Amphitheatre,'" explains the guide who accompanied the car. "You will notice that as we ascend those mountains seem to rise one after another and follow us." We did notice them; we were looking right at them and couldn't help it. It was an optical illusion that was rather startling. We thought at first that the mountains would overtake us, but they didn't. "This is 'Granite Gorge,'" continues the guide, as we enter a great cut that rears its granite walls on

ECHO MOUNTAIN HOUSE AND CAR ON THE 48 PER CENT. GRADE, MT. LOWE RAILWAY.

either side of us and lose sight of the mountains that are chasing us. "The workmen on this road were eight months in hewing this passage through these rocks, and before a tie or rail was laid they had to clamber to these rugged heights and carry their implements with them, and much of the material used in the construction of the road, such as water, cement, and lumber, had to be carried on the backs of burros and on the shoulders of men. This bridge that we are now crossing is called the MacPherson Trestle, and there is no other bridge like it in the world. It is 200 feet long and 100 feet higher at one end than the other. If it were not for the clouds you could obtain a good scenic view from here." Clouds! We had not thought of it before, so interested were we in the talk of our guide, but we notice now that the sun is shining, and looking up we see no vestige of a cloud in the bright, blue sky above.

Looking again, beneath and beyond us, such a sight meets our gaze as our eyes had never rested on before. A vast white sea of billowy vapor overhangs the great San Gabriel Valley and hides it from our view. This alone is worth the trip to see—an immense heaving sea of clouds, an ocean of fleecy vapor billows that surge and roll and toss as though seeking for a shore of sand and rock upon which to spend their restless force. Halting at the summit of the great cable incline, we find we have arrived at the Echo Mountain House, where we change cars, taking an electric road called the Alpine Division of the Mt. Lowe Railway, which extends from Echo Mountain to Mt. Lowe Springs, where "Ye Alpine Tavern" is located.

As we board the Alpine Division observation car I

again cast my eyes over toward the San Gabriel Valley, where a few minutes before we had beheld the battle of the clouds. What a grand transformation! The clouds have been dispersed as though by magic, and lying spread out in the valley 3500 feet beneath us is a panorama of such incomparable and inconceivable beauty and loveliness that we gaze for a moment enraptured, speechless, spellbound, dazed. They must be all looking, for there hasn't been a word uttered for a minute. I am feasting my eyes on the supreme beauty of the scenery and drinking deeply at the fountain of delight; at the same time I'm trying to count the squares in the city of Pasadena and the orange groves that dot the valley. "It's all there, but it's a good ways off," remarks Charlie Sloane, breaking the spell of silence. "My gracious! isn't that fine? It beats looking across Jersey through the crown of Billy Penn's hat," exclaims George Alfalfa in a guarded tone.

The electric current is turned on, our car starts quietly off, and for four miles we pass over the most wonderfully constructed railway in the world. We do not go very fast—in fact, we would rather not, for taking everything into consideration this is not very good ground for "scorching," and going at a gentle, easy pace lessens our chances of being rolled a few thousand feet down the side of a mountain. Not that any of us are afraid of being "dumped"; we didn't come up here to be scared, but out of curiosity to see what it is like, and the more slowly the car moves the better able we are to see and the longer we can look at what we do see.

This entire roadbed, hewn out of the sides of the mountain, forms a solid granite ledge upon which the

MT. LOWE RAILWAY, CALIFORNIA.

road is built, and it is always a towering wall of rock on one side and a yawning chasm on the other. To this there is but one exception, the "Grand Circular Bridge." From this structure you can look from both sides down into the depths. If you don't want to look you can shut your eyes.

Professor Lowe has constructed this railway at a cost of many hundred thousand dollars to enable tourists to penetrate the heart of the Sierra Madre Mountain, that they may form some conception of what an isolated mountain wilderness is like. It is all here and ever-present, in boundless, grand profusion—mountains, wilderness, isolation—an awe-inspiring, infinite trinity of grandeur, that almost makes your head swim and your heart stand still. Our tracks shelve the very summit of the sloping walls of mighty cañons, and you can look down 3000 feet into their wooded depths.

We arrive in due time at Mt. Lowe Springs, the terminus of the road, and are 5000 feet above the level of the sea. From here we can see the summit of Mt. Lowe, two miles away and 1000 feet above us. It is intended to extend the tracks to this point in the near future. A bridle path leads to it, and you can make the trip now on the back of a burro. A pathway leads to "Inspiration Point," half a mile away, from which it is said magnificent views can be had. Our time is limited; we hasten to the famous spring, drink of its ice-cold water, and then visit the homelike, cozy club house, "Ye Alpine Tavern," and give it a hurried inspection.

Nestling among giant oaks and pines, it occupies a romantic and picturesque location; in style of architecture it is attractive and unique, being something on the order of a Swiss chalet. It is two and a half stories in height, with ground dimensions of 40 by 80 feet; contains 20 bed rooms, a large dining room, billiard hall, and kitchen. It is built of granite and Oregon pine, finished in the natural color of the wood. The design of the main hall or dining room is the most striking feature connected with the construction of the building. Artistically located around the room in uniform order are five cheerful open fireplaces, in the largest of which swings a mammoth iron pot on a huge crane. It is 7 feet high and 12 feet wide. Blocks of granite have been placed in its corners for seats, and over the mantel above it is the somewhat flattering but old-time hospitable inscription, "YE ORNAMENT OF A HOUSE IS YE GUEST WHO DOTH FREQUENT IT." On one side of this mantel is a brick oven of ancient design; on the other side is a receptacle of peculiar and unique construction and suspicious appearance, which no doubt contains the liquid nourishment of the establishment.

"I wonder what they keep in this funny-looking cupboard," whispers Brother Kilgore in my ear, as we were looking around in the dining room.

"Suppose we look and see," I reply, as I attempt to open the door. "No, you don't; it's fastened. I'll see who's got the key," is the rejoinder as he hurriedly walks away. Passing outside, I notice a number of the party are getting aboard the car, and as I join them the motorman shouts "All aboard." "Are our people all here?" asks Manager Wyman, as he casts his eyes over the crowd. "Brother Denniston isn't here. I think he went to Inspiration Point," replies Brother Barrett. "Nor Brother Kilgore," I add. "He went to look for a

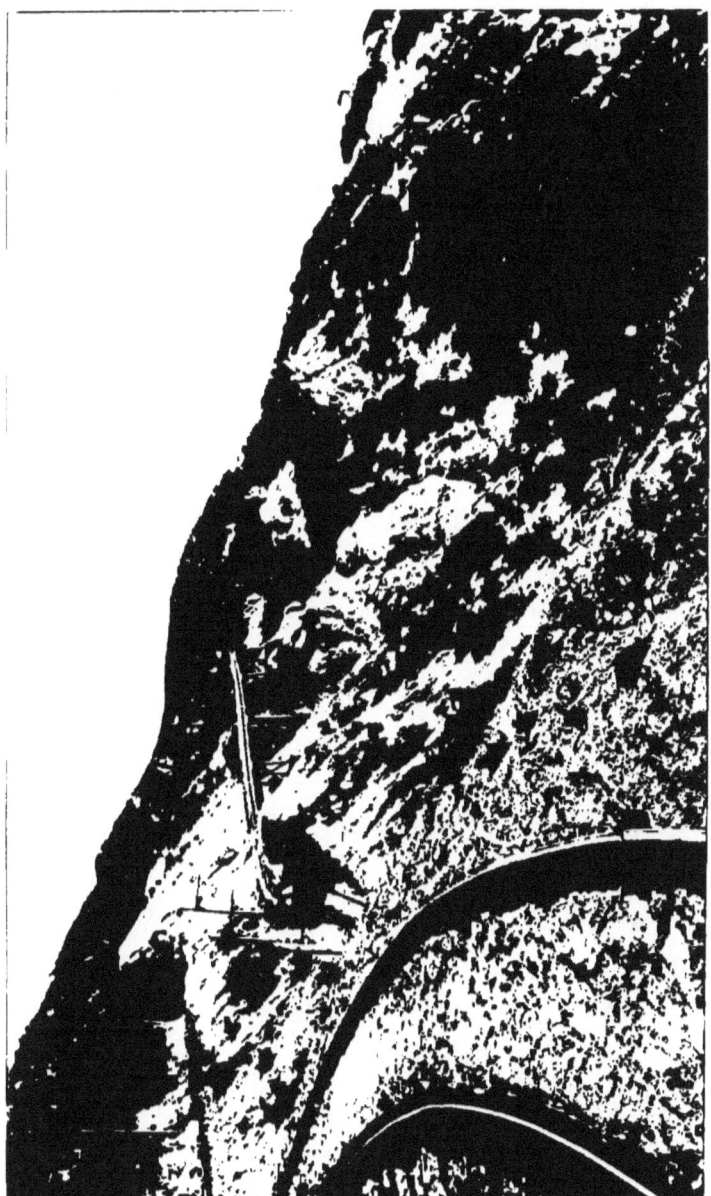

CIRCULAR BRIDGE, MT. LOWE RAILWAY, CALIFORNIA.

man with a key." "I'm here," says Brother Kilgore, as he emerges from the door of the "Tavern," wiping his mouth in a suspicious manner; at the same time Brother Denniston and his "company" are seen coming from toward the "spring" and soon we are "all aboard" and "homeward bound." At one point on our descent three or four mountain goats are seen on the track ahead of us, but on our approach they quickly disappear from sight in the thicket. It is with difficulty that Brothers Sloane and Haas can be restrained from leaping overboard and giving chase. Thirty minutes stop at Echo Mountain gives us an opportunity of visiting the beautiful hotel at this point, the "Echo Mountain House," which is located on the summit of Echo Mountain and is said to be one of the finest equipped mountain hotels in the world. From its veranda and balcony hundreds of visitors daily view with rapture and delight the wonderful scenery of the San Gabriel Valley and its surroundings. A small cannon fired off on the lawn has a startling effect, and proves that the mountain is not misnamed. The report echoes from peak to peak and then seems to go bounding and tumbling down the cañons and ravines, growing fainter and fainter until it gradually dies away in the distance.

The great "World's Fair search light," purchased by Professor Lowe and established on Echo Mountain, is operated nightly for the pleasure and entertainment of visitors. The power of its light is that of 3,000,000 candles and its rays can be seen for 150 miles on the Pacific Ocean. Its beams falling upon a newspaper 35 miles away will enable a person to easily read it. Our time is up, and boarding the "White Chariot" we commence our descent of the great cable incline, reaching the bottom in safety. A photographer is on hand and "pressed the button" on the car and contents.

On our trip to and fro to-day we passed in sight of the beautiful home of Professor Lowe, near Pasadena, and returning I had the pleasure and honor of meeting and conversing with him during the twenty minutes we rode together on the Pasadena and Los Angeles Electric Railway. I was introduced to the professor by Brother Edward Butcher, and we took a seat together. He is a large man of fine appearance and carries himself with the graceful mien of a brigadier-general; his eye is bright and kind, his voice gentle and agreeable, and we are the best of friends in a minute. "Professor," I remarked, "there are but a very few of the people, I warrant, who ascend that marvelous cable incline, who enjoy the pleasure and excitement of that unequaled ride among the wild, magnificent mountain scenery of your Alpine Division on a comfortable trolley car, that ever give a second thought to the men who endured hardships and risked their lives to even survey a road like that. I have thought of this several times to-day, and would like to ask how you ever induced men to traverse those cliffs and peaks and cañon walls, where a mountain goat can hardly secure a footing?" "Well," answered the professor, "you know there are no hardships so severe they will not be endured, no risks so great they will not be taken, if only men have a leader to follow and are well paid for following him. Long before a measurement was taken or a stake was driven, when the idea that such a road were possible first entered my mind, I spent many days with only an employed attendant my companion,

YE ALPINE TAVERN, MT. LOWE, CALIFORNIA.

in making my way from Rubio Cañon to the crest of the highest peak along the route which you traveled with so much pleasure to-day in less than 90 minutes. I headed every surveying party that went out in the interest of the enterprise. I have personally directed all the operations that have required engineering skill and experience; I have expended almost one and a half millions of dollars, and my work isn't completed yet." "That is an enormous sum of money to invest in a venture, or rather an experiment, that you don't know will pay till you try it," I ventured to assert, while secretly admiring the indomitable courage and spirit of the man. "Yes, it is a great deal of money," was the reply, and I imagined that a sigh accompanied the words. "As a financial scheme I believe it will be a failure. I have no hope of ever getting out of it what money I have put in it, but to me this is only a secondary matter. I've watched a vague visionary dream grow into a bright reality; I've had cherished theories, condemned as insane and impracticable, converted into substantial facts; I have solved the greatest engineering and mechanical problems that ever taxed the brain of man; I've won the hardest, toughest intellectual battle that ever was fought; I've had an all-absorbing ambition gratified, and I feel that I have, in a measure, got the worth of my money." As the professor ceased speaking there was a bright look in his eye and a happy expression on his countenance as though it were a great pleasure to reflect on the great work he had accomplished. The car was approaching his destination; he arose to go and extended his hand. As I took it he said, "When you come again you can extend your ride to the summit of the mountain, for I propose to complete the work in a short time; and you must stay longer, for in your hurried trip to-day there is much you didn't see, and I would wish that you could see it all; goodbye." The car stopped and he was gone. As he disappeared from view I said to myself, "There goes a wonderful man."

Continuing a few blocks further we left the car and visited the Chamber of Commerce and spent half an hour among its interesting relics and curiosities. When we reach our train the most of our people are there, the time for starting being almost up. We bid adieu to the kind friends we have made while here, and who did all they could to make our short stay a pleasant one, and at 5.00 P. M. Eastern (2.00 P. M. Pacific) we pull out of the station at Los Angeles bound for San Francisco and the "Golden Gate," 482 miles away.

We are still on the Southern Pacific's famous "Sunset Route," which we have followed since leaving Sierra Blanca. S. P. engine No. 1826 is pulling us, with Engineer Charlie Hill at the throttle. She is fired by E. Homes, who has a hard task on hand, for there are steep grades to climb and our train is heavy. William Perkins is conducting the train; the brakemen are J. B. Freet and F. W. Bunnell. These three gentlemen are brothers of the "Order" and members of El Capitan Division No. 115, of San Francisco. They are members of the entertainment committee from that division and have been selected to run our train that they may be able to look after our welfare. J. C. Fielding, also a member of El Capitan Division and of the committee, is a guest on the train, along with Brother Twist,

T. S. C. LOWE.

of Golden Gate Division No. 364, of Oakland, Cal., also a member of the committee.

Following the course of Los Angeles River as we leave the "City of Angels" behind us, we pass for quite a distance through a fine farming country, where hundreds of acres of barley are being gathered for hay into great heaps and stacks.

"Brother Freet," I ask, as we sit near the wide-open door of the baggage compartment looking out on the fleeting landscape, "do they feed their stock altogether on barley hay in California?" "Not entirely. What makes you think so?" is the inquiring answer. "It looks so from the fact that in all the arable country we have passed through since entering this State, outside of fruit and flower culture, I have noticed no other product than barley, with the exception of a few patches of alfalfa grass," I reply. "You are right," is the response, "so far as concerns that part of the country you have seen; although if you traverse the State from end to end you will see comparatively little of it. There are sections of California where abundant crops of corn are raised, but while it has never achieved distinction as a corn producing State, it is second to no State in the Union in its yield of wheat. The entire area of the State of Indiana would be insufficient to cover the wheat fields of California, which yielded last year almost 40,000,000 bushels; but speaking of barley, cut as it is in a green state after the grain has formed and cured for hay, it makes a valuable and nourishing food for stock, upon which they will fatten without additional grain feed."

Since leaving Los Angeles our course has been upward, and now as we pass the little station of Fernando, we are close to the San Fernando Range, 25 miles northwest of Los Angeles and over 1100 feet above it. A tunnel one and one-quarter miles in length pierces the above-named range, and into this we now plunge. It is a dark hole, an undesirable place to be; our train runs slowly, and the cars become filled with smoke and gas that is almost suffocating; we do no talking and as little breathing as possible for an interval of ten or twelve minutes, when we again emerge into the open air and sunshine and breathe freely once more. We have left the scenes of agricultural industry behind us and again enter a region of unproductive sterility and aridity. We pass through the little town of Saugus, from which place a branch road runs to Santa Barbara, yet the country don't improve. We are strongly reminded of the Colorado Desert: alkali dust, glaring sand, stunted sage brush, and cactus on every hand. The elevation here is about 3000 feet higher than the Colorado Desert, but the conditions seem about the same.

Midway between Saugus and Mojave we enter the western border of the Great Mojave Desert, which we follow for several miles; here we are treated to novel, interesting, and remarkable scenery. On the right as far as the range of vision extends stretches the vast Mojave Desert, with its lavish growth of magnificent giant cactus, many of them from 25 to 40 feet in height, with branched and bushy tops, from the centre of which in many cases can be seen protruding an immense pinkish bloom.

This great desert, with its wonderful and peculiar

plant life, extends, we are told, away off hundreds of miles into Nevada and Arizona. On the left the scenery is different. You gaze off and across the great Antelope Valley, 80 miles in width, level as a floor and almost devoid of tree or bush. It looks brown and barren, but we are informed it is considered good grazing territory. The grass, though dead and dry at certain seasons of the year, like that of the San Simon Valley in Arizona, retains all its nutritious qualities and flavor, and stock feed upon it with apparent relish.

Owing to unfavorable natural conditions and surroundings, it is hardly expected that we will encounter a very extensive population, but what few people we do meet who are residents of the country are principally employees of the railroad company, around whose stations usually cluster a group of snug and neat-looking cottages built by the company for the use of the men and their families. Good water can be obtained at a reasonable depth, and wind mills are used for pumping. Patches of ground are irrigated and cultivated, upon which are grown flowers, fruit, and vegetables. Our train slows up and stops for water at one of these oases in the desert, and looking out the window I discover that it is quite a town. A number of our people have left the train and are looking around.

Alighting from the train in front of the station I look up and see the old familiar homelike name of Lancaster above the door. Everything bears evidence of thrift and good living, even to an almost empty ice-cream can that sits inside the waiting-room door, and which, with other things, is being inspected and investigated. Time is up, "All aboard" is shouted, we scramble on, and as the train moves off Brother Houston, who is fast in the ice-cream can, came near being left. At Mojave, another thrifty town of considerable size, where connections are made with the Atlantic and Pacific Railway, our train stops to attach a helper engine. After a delay of five minutes we resume our journey, assisted by Engineer Cain and Fireman Curren with engine No. 1808.

As we leave Mojave it is growing dusk, and by the time we reach the summit of the grade and stop at Tehachapi it has become quite dark. This we all exceedingly regret, for we are now about to enter upon the most wonderful and interesting 33 miles of road on the whole Southern Pacific system, where we drop from an elevation of 4025 feet to that of 672. Making the descent of 3553 feet requires an almost continual application of the air brakes, which heats the brake shoes red hot and makes the fire fly. We feel concerned and wish we could see. We know at one time we are going around a sharp curve and at another time pitching down a grade much steeper than usual, and very often we find we are doing both at one and the same time. We look out of the window on one side and see a towering mountain wall, so near you can touch it with your hand; we look out on the other side, and see nothing, only a seemingly illimitable depth, filled with darkness and uncertainty; and this is the grand, picturesque Tehachapi Pass, whose sinuous windings, devious ways, complex maneuvering, and bewildering curves compels the railroad to run over top and underneath itself, forming the extraordinary famous Loop.

We had heard much of it, and we all expected to see it; our only hope and desire now is to get safely away from it and beyond it to straight track and level country once more. All good things must have an ending, and bad things can't last forever, so the novelty and excitement of our toboggan-like mountain ride and its two hours' suspense is over as our train stops at Bakersfield, where another change of engines is made.

It is now past midnight in Philadelphia, 12.50 A. M.; at Bakersfield it is only 9.50 P. M., but many of our people are retiring, for it has been a day fraught with pleasure and excitement, wearing both on the mind and body, and we all need rest and plenty of it to prepare us for the approaching morrow. "Captain," I said, as Brother Perkins came down the curtained aisle of the "Marco," while I was wrestling with a refractory collar button preparing to turn in, "will you kindly give me the number of the engine that is drawing us and the names of the engineer and fireman? I am trying to keep a record of the engines and crews that handle us, and I don't wish to miss any." "Certainly," is the response; "we have engine No. 1417 that runs to Mendota, 140 miles; the engineer's and fireman's names are Cole; the Cole Boys we call them—good, lively fellows." "With two live Coles in the cab and lots of them in the firebox, I guess we will reach Mendota on time," came the smothered comment in a drowsy tone from the berth of Manager Wyman.

### FRIDAY, MAY 21st.

Awakened this morning about six o'clock by Mrs. S., always an early riser, who exclaims, "Get up! get up! we're almost there." "Almost where, my dear?" I sleepily inquire. "I don't know where, but Mr. Terry,

Mr. Brown, Mr. Horner, and Mr. Springer are all up, and they say we are nearly there," she answers. I turn over, raise the blind, and look out of the window. "And Mr. McDonald says we're going to have an early breakfast," she adds, as she retreats down the aisle. That last information she knows will fetch me if nothing else will, but I'm still looking out of the window wondering where we are; thought at first we had lost our way in the intricate descent of the Tehachapi Range, got tangled up in the Loop, turned around, and were again entering Los Angeles.

What magic had been at work during the night? The world outside is teeming with verdant vegetation. Fruit-laden trees, rose-burdened bushes, green grass, and flowers everywhere. I quickly roll out of my berth and dress, or rather I nearly roll out of my berth while quickly dressing, for one inconvenience of this way of living is, you've got to dress and then get out of bed, watching yourself very closely that you don't involuntarily get out before you're ready, for when, with one leg in your pants and about to put the other one in, your car hits a curve, *look out*.

The first person I meet as I enter the smoker is the conductor who is running the train. "Good morning, captain; where are we?" I ask. "We are entering Port Costa, 25 miles from Oakland," he answers. "Have you time to give me the number of your engine and the names of your crew?" I inquire, with every-ready notebook in hand, as he was about turning away, for the train is stopping at the station. "We left Mendota this morning at two o'clock with engine No. 1408, Engineer Edwards, Fireman Duran, Brakemen Owen and Todd,

GEORGE W. BROWN, OF THE COMMITTEE.

and my name is Schu," he hurriedly said as he left the car and enters the telegraph office. In a short time Conductor Schu comes out of the office with train orders and our train is soon on its way again.

At 10.30 A. M. Eastern (7.30 Pacific) we reach Oakland (Sixteenth Street), where we lay for an hour and a half. It is a tedious wait. We cannot leave the train, for we do not know at what minute it might conclude to go, and none of us want to get left. We stroll around, first on one side of the train and then on the other, keeping one eye on it for fear it will get away from us and careful not to get too far out of its reach. We can see that Oakland is a large and beautiful city, and learn that it has a population of 60,000 inhabitants; a place where flowers bloom on the lawns, fruits mature in the orchards, vegetables grow in the gardens, and grains are harvested in the fields each and every month in the year. It has mountain scenery back of it and an ocean view in front of it; another blooming paradise where desolating storms are unknown and frosts and snows are never seen.

Finding our train about to move we all get aboard and in a few minutes are landed at Oakland Pier, where we wait half an hour for a boat to convey us eight miles across the bay to San Francisco. We employ the time in looking about the large, commodious waiting room that overlooks the harbor. We can't help noticing that this apartment contains something that is never seen in a station waiting room on the Pennsylvania Railroad system. A profusion of advertisements of all kinds literally cover the walls, and occupying a space in the centre of the floor is a large glass case containing a pyramid of bottles filled with liquors of various kinds and brands, advertising the goods of a whiskey firm down on Front Street. It is needless to say that there is a railing around the exhibit and the door of the case is locked. One of the ticket collectors, an active old gentleman, quick in his movements as a boy, informs us that he has been in his present position for nineteen years; and although seventy years old, the climate is so healthy he feels that he is growing younger every day.

It is announced that the boat is now ready, and we "walk the plank" leading to the deck of the "Oakland," which is soon plowing a furrow in the waters of the bay as she heads for the "Queen City" of the Pacific. It is not such a boat ride as one can term "lovely"; it is not even agreeable. A chilly gale sweeps the deck that almost lifts you off your feet. "Golly, it's worse than a trip from Camden to Philadelphia in December," exclaims Brother Goff, as he turns up the collar of his coat. "Or one from Jersey City to New York in February," adds Brother McKernan, seeking refuge behind a post. The most of us retire to the more comfortable quarters of the cabin, where we find enjoyment in viewing from the windows the immense bay and harbor, where are anchored hundreds of vessels of all kinds and sizes. As the "Oakland" pokes her nose against the San Francisco dock I look at my watch; it is 9.55 A. M., Pacific time. We have just been twenty minutes coming across. A speed of a mile in two and a half minutes is a pretty lively gait for a ferryboat, but we are told the "Oakland" does it every trip. Under the escort of Brother Perkins, we are loaded into cable cars and start on our way to Sutro Garden and Golden Gate Park.

I believe there's hardly three squares of a level street in the whole city of San Francisco. Such hills as we go up and such hills as we go down we never saw in any city before. "Why, this is ten times worse than Baltimore, and it's bad enough, dear knows," exclaims Mrs. Kalkman as she catches Brother Cohee around the neck to save herself from falling off the seat as the car shoots up an unusually steep acclivity. "Here, here, don't be so affectionate; Brother Kalkman and Mrs. Cohee are looking at you," warns Brother Cohee. "As if I'd hug you on purpose," she retorts, giving him a look of scorn. In many streets a horse and wagon has never been seen; it would be impossible for a horse to draw a wagon up those abrupt granite-paved hills. With the cable car almost on end, we are descending one of those "shoot the chute" like declivities extending for about three blocks, when I overhear a passenger, evidently a resident of the neighborhood, say to Mrs. Shaw, who has "struck up" a conversation with her, "We had a fire here in our neighborhood a short time ago, and a driver of one of the fire engines tried to bring it down this hill, when one of the horses fell down and the engine ran over it and killed it, and it broke the engine all up and hurt the man; it was just awful." The car stops at the next corner and the woman gets off; glancing back at the hill we have just descended her closing words, "just awful," strike me as being very appropriate.

A few squares further and we abandon the cable cars and take a little steam road called the "Ferries and Cliff" Railroad that carries us to Sutro Park and bathing pavilion, owned by Adolph Sutro, a retired millionaire merchant of San Francisco, and to the celebrated

Cliff House, near which are the far-famed Seal Rocks. We wandered for a time through the beautifully laid out statuary, shrubbery, and flower-adorned grounds of Sutro, then to the great pavilion, that not only contains a large museum of interesting relics and curiosities, but it is here that the noted Sutro baths are located, said to be the finest equipped artificial bathing pools in the world.

We cannot stand the temptation, and soon many of us are robed in bathing suits and are diving, plunging, rolling, and splashing in the salt waters of the Pacific, brought here and warmed to the proper temperature, permitting bathing to be indulged in the entire year. It is needless to say that we have lots of sport, and those who decline to indulge will regret it. There are several strangers in the pool, and Brother Sheppard has taken quite a fancy to one young fellow, whom he is trying to learn to swim and dive. In an adjoining pool is rather a forlorn-looking duck; it must be tame, for it is quietly swimming around undisturbed by the noise we make. "I think it's hungry," says Brother McCarty, "I wish I had some crumbs." The creature must have heard him, for we imagine it gave him a grateful look.

From the baths we go to the Cliff House, and from the windows of the inclosed balcony, that almost overhangs the waves that dash and roar on the rocks beneath, we watch with interest the monster seals that by the hundreds climb and crawl and slip and slide over the crags that rise from the bay, while we regale ourselves with pork and beans and coffee. There is a strong, chilly wind blowing, and we do not tarry long on the bluff outside that overlooks the bay and seals.

It is twenty minutes past two as we get aboard a train on the Park and Ocean Railroad that will convey us to Golden Gate Park. We do not find this world-famed park very different in appearance from other parks we have seen. It is all nice—very nice; beautiful trees and plants and shrubbery, velvety green grass and bright blooming flowers, fine fountains and lakes of shimmering water. All this we see and enjoy, but we have seen the like before, time and time again. Some are bold enough to so express themselves, and it catches Brother Perkins' ear, who good-naturedly says, "My dear friends, there is but one Golden Gate Park in all the world. There are 1040 acres here of as fine a park as there is anywhere under the sun, and when we consider that 25 years ago this was all a barren tract of drifting sand hills, that everything you see growing has been planted and is kept alive and green and blooming by a regular and almost constant application of water, when you remember this, then you will feel and think that this park is a little different from any other that you have seen."

We had already commenced to think it was. Amongst groves of trees are great inclosures containing native buffalo, elk, and deer, with so much room to roam that they hardly feel the restraint of captivity. We enter the immense aviaries, where many varieties of birds and squirrels flit and chirp and scamper and chatter with all the freedom and unconcern of an unlimited out-door life. As we leave this great cage with its sprightly, vociferous occupants I hear Brother Reilly say, "McCarty has got a 'mash.'" I don't quite know what it is that Brother McCarty has got, but suppose it is some escaped animal or bird he has captured. I turn and look, to find him surrounded by ladies of our party, who seem to be trying to protect him from impending harm. Looking closer, I see disappearing among the shrubbery McCarty's "mash," the cause of all the trouble, and it is only the poor bedraggled duck of Sutro's bath that Brother McCarty had thought looked hungry, and our ladies had scared it off. Brother Reagan would have recaptured it but for Miss Ella's restraining hand, and the curiosity is lost.

We are all pretty tired when at last the street cars are boarded and we are on our way to the ferry. Some are going to return to our train, which lies in Oakland, and some will remain in this city. Mrs. S. and myself called on Mrs. David Chambers, who, with her son and daughter, Willie and Effie, live on Mission Street. Years ago Mrs. Chambers and her family were neighbors to us in West Chester, Pa. Willie, when but a lad, was advised to try the climate of the Pacific coast for his health. He found both health and lucrative employment. Ten years ago he sent East for his mother and sister. We find them to-day enjoying excellent health and nicely and comfortably fixed. We are given a warm, cordial welcome and persuaded to spend the night with them.

In the evening after dinner Willie took me out to see the town. The ladies declined to go, preferring to remain indoors and talk over old times. Met Leslie Collom, a young gentleman friend of the Chambers', but he having other engagements could not go. Willie knows the town and I follow where he leads. It has long been a desire with me to see San Francisco's

"*Chinatown,*" and for three hours we explore its darkness and its mysteries. We do not attempt to go very far up and we don't try to get very far down—we steer about on a level; but we see enough to convince me that Chinatown is all that it is said to be. You don't have to ascend into rickety, reeking lofts or descend into gloomy, foul dens to witness their degradation, weakness, and misery; far back in dark, forbidding alleys and bystreets, which make your flesh creep to traverse, you can find them huddled together on benches and shelves, like chickens on a roost, enveloped in disgusting, stupefying smoke.

On our way home we dropped into a private museum and saw one of the rarest and most wonderful pieces of Japanese art in the world, a realistic, life-size statue of a man carved from wood. It is claimed that this work has been examined by learned scientific men, skilled in anatomy and physiology, and not a line or lineament of the skin surface of the human body has been omitted in this delicate, intricate carving. The finger nails are there and all the fine lines that can be traced on the inside of the hand and fingers. There are many lines on the surface of the human body that require the aid of a magnifying glass to discern; with the glass all these lines can be seen carved on this wonderful piece of art. It is midnight when we get home, and, thoroughly tired, we are soon in bed and in the land of dreams.

## SATURDAY, MAY 22d.

Arose this morning about half-past six, and after breakfast, accompanied by Leslie Collom, went to the Palace Hotel, where we met Brothers Wyman and Layfield with their ladies. Brother Wyman had planned a trip to San José and was expecting others of the party, but a number of them being exhausted, worn out by an all night's effort to explore the length, breadth, height, and depth of Chinatown, were still in bed. The others were too much interested in the beautiful city of Oakland and its environments to come, for we hear the good people over there are showing them a royal time, the municipal authorities giving them the freedom of the city and the railway company the freedom of their lines. Finding that no others are coming, we six board a Southern Pacific train on the Coast Division, that extends from San Francisco to Monterey, bound for San José, a ride of fifty miles. Mr. Collom is a very much appreciated member of our little party, as he points out from time to time much that interests us. As the train pulls out through the city he shows us the church where Blanche Lamont and Minnie Williams were found murdered and a little further on he points out the house where Durrant, the convicted murderer had lived.

The road runs between the ocean and the bay and as we pass the station of Ocean View a broad expanse of the Pacific greets our vision. At Baden we get pretty close to the shore of the bay and follow it until we leave Burlingame, a distance of about eight miles. We pass Menlo Park and Palo Alto, when our attention is called by Mr. Collom to a group of low-built, red-roofed, substantial-looking buildings, a short distance from the road on our right, almost hidden from view by the trees that cluster about them. "That," says Mr. Collom, "is the renowned Leland Stanford University, founded in 1885 by the multi-millionaire Leland Stanford and his wife as a monument to the memory of their only child, Leland, Jr., who had died a short time before. Eighty-three thousand acres of land, valued at $20,000,000, was dedicated by a deed of trust for the establishment of this institution. Mr. Stanford selected the site for the location of the buildings, and the corner stone was laid in 1887, ten years ago. Last year the school register showed an enrollment of 1100 pupils. Tuition is free, both males and females are admitted, and the students are from all parts of America."

As we leave Mountain View Station Mr. Collom suggests that we now give the scenery on the left of the train our attention, at the same time pointing out in the far distance a mountain peak, saying, "San José is 10 miles from here, and almost on a direct line with this point, and the crest of that mountain, 30 miles away, is Mt. Hamilton, where the famous Lick Observatory is located. It has an elevation of almost 4500 feet, and if you only had time to go up there it is a trip worth taking."

Leaving Santa Clara Station we pass near a large, fine park, among the trees of which can be seen beautiful, substantial buildings. "That is Santa Clara Female College," said Mr. Collom.

The train now enters San José, and we alight at the station. A "Vendome" hack is in waiting, which we enter, and are driven to that superb hostelry, said to be one of the finest hotels in California. It is situated in the centre of a beautiful 12-acre park, only a short distance from the railroad station. Not having long to stay, after a few minutes rest we bid the genial host good-day and start out for a little walk.

"We will return by the narrow-gauge road," says

Brother Wyman, "if we can find the station." "A man told me a little while ago that it is only five blocks over in this direction," replies the Colonel, indicating with his finger the way we should go. "Yes, the narrow-gauge road runs through that part of the town, but I think you will find it farther than five blocks," remarks Mr. Collom. "Well, we want to see the town, anyway, and we'll take our time," responded the Colonel. "This is a pretty large town as well as a pretty old one, is it not, Mr. Collom?" I ask. "Yes," is the answer. "It was first settled when Santa Clara Mission was founded, 120 years ago. It has now a population of about 25,000, and is the county seat of Santa Clara County, one of the richest counties in agricultural products and fruits in the State. Because of the wealth of fertility surrounding it San José has long been known as the 'Garden City' of California."

Sauntering along, with our eyes wide open for the sights of the town, and keeping as much in the shade as possible, for the sun shines very warm, we are getting all the enjoyment out of the situation possible; but things are becoming less interesting. We are all hungry and the ladies are becoming tired; we have already come seven blocks, and the Colonel says, "We are nearly there; but to be sure of it I will ask this man," he adds, as a man leading a horse came around the corner toward us. "My good man," says the Colonel, "can you tell us how far it is to the narrow-gauge railroad station from here?" "Yes, sir; 'bout five blocks," is the answer. "You're sure it's not ten?" retorts Brother Wyman; but the man and horse, never stopping, were out of range, and the shot missed the mark.

"I'm hungry," exclaims Mrs. Wyman. "So am I," I add. "I guess we can all eat if we have a chance," asserts Brother Wyman. "We'll look for a restaurant," says the Colonel. A walk of two squares farther brings us to the looked-for establishment, which we enter, and after partaking of a substantial lunch, I ask the man at the desk, and I try to do it without feeling or agitation, making just the plain, quiet inquiry, "Will you tell us, please, how far it is to the narrow-gauge railroad station?" "Five blocks straight ahead," is the pleasant, quiet reply, as he waves his hand in the direction we are to go. Not a word from one of our party. I take a second look at the man to see if I can discover in that pleasant countenance the least shadow of deception; it is as innocent and guileless as the face of day.

We silently leave the place, and as we start up the street Mrs. Layfield, taking the Colonel's arm, gently asks, "John, are we going to walk to San Francisco?" "Not if we can find the station," says the Colonel.

We enter the large store of a wine merchant to look around, and are courteously treated by the gentlemanly proprietor, who gave the ladies each a bottle of wine. We have come four blocks and a half since lunch and are looking for the station, when suddenly the Colonel exclaims, "There's the road; I thought that last fellow was telling the truth." "But that's not the road we want; that's a trolley road," replies Brother Wyman. "So it is," admits the Colonel; "but there's a man; I'll ask him," he adds, referring to a man in uniform who was leaning up against the fence.

"For Lord's sake," pleads the Colonel, "will you tell us how far it is to the narrow-gauge railroad station?"

"About a square and a half," answers the man, smiling at the Colonel's earnestness. "Are you sure it's no further than that?" asks the Colonel. "Quite sure," is the reply. "How soon can we get a train for San Francisco?" inquires Manager Wyman. "In about an hour and a half. Where're you from?" he answers and asks at the same time. "From Philadelphia, Pennsylvania. Where's your road go?" imitates Brother Wyman. The man laughs. "I'm unable to take you home, for I don't go that far," he replies, "but I can take you several miles and back through as fine a fruit country as you ever saw. I am waiting to relieve the man on the car you see coming, and in a few minutes I will be going back. The fare is only a nickel," he adds, as a hint that we musn't expect to "deadhead" it.

We conclude to go, to pass the time away, for we can easily get back in time to catch our train. So we get aboard the car, pay our nickel, and ride for several miles to a place called the Willows, which is the terminus of the road. Here is located an immense cherry orchard, where the crop is being gathered and crated ready for shipment to Eastern markets.

We are invited to help ourselves; it is half an hour before our car starts back and we have time to accept the invitation. The ripest cherries are the ones the packers reject, so we assisted the packers for several minutes picking out the ripe cherries and packing them while the packers packed the ones we didn't pick. When we got tired of packing we quit picking, and thanking the good people for the treat, we board the car again and are soon spinning up the line among the apricot and cherry orchards, the trees loaded with fruit.

Arriving at our destination, we bid our friend, the conductor, goodbye, and in a few minutes we reach the much-inquired-for "narrow-gauge railroad station," where we wait half an hour for the train. We find the track composed of three rails; and as though to demonstrate to us the use of the third rail, a freight train comes along made up of both narrow and broad-gauge cars. It looks odd, for it is something we had never seen before, and as the strange combination passes down the road the Colonel remarks, "There is nothing but what we may expect to see."

In due time our train pulls into the station and we are soon seated in a comfortable narrow-gauge coach and speeding toward Oakland. There are many beautiful towns and residences located on this line, and as we draw nearer its termination this fact becomes more noticeable, the town of Alameda, through which we pass, possessing all the loveliness of a fairyland with its palatial residences and magnificent lawns.

Oakland, the "Athens of the Pacific," is reached at last, and knowing how fascinating and grand it is and how royally our people are being treated, I am loath to leave; but our friends on the other side await our coming, and bidding the manager, the Colonel, and the ladies good night, Mr. Collom and I hie away to the ferry and across the bay, nor stop until we are seated in Mrs. Chambers' cozy dining room, appeasing our appetites while recounting the incidents of the day. After dinner Willie took his mother, Mrs. Shaw, and myself out to give us a view of the city lights from "Park Heights." A ride on the cable cars and several changes brought us in about forty minutes to the "Heights."

From this high eminence we look down on a sight of unusual novelty and grandeur. Spread out far beneath us is almost the entire city of San Francisco, but the buildings are not visible, not one, only the millions of bright, star-like lights that enable you to trace the streets and mark the squares, and that twinkle and gleam from beneath like unto the gems that beam down upon you from above. We look up, through a cloudless atmosphere, and behold a firmament filled with brilliant, glittering gems; we look down, and see what almost seems a reflection of what we see above. Man, we know, is the author of all this grandeur that we see beneath, but as to the Author of that magnificence far above we can but speculate.

Willie sees we are growing serious and says we need a change, so he leads us around to the entrance that admits to the scenic railway, chutes, haunted swing, and skating rink, where for an hour we have a world of fun; so pleased are the ladies with the toboggan and the chutes that it is with difficulty we get them started home. We have had another full day, and when at eleven o'clock I find myself in bed, I discover that I am very tired. After the excitement and exertions of the day are over, when the tension and strain of overtaxed nerves and muscles relax and reaction comes, then you understand in its fullest measure the meaning of the expression, "I'm tired."

### SUNDAY, MAY 23d.

Feeling that we need rest, and finding the full enjoyment of our need in the pleasant home of Mrs. Chambers, we do not go out to-day until it is time to leave

JOHN H. REAGAN, OF THE COMMITTEE.

for the ferry, from which the boat will bear us to Oakland and to our train, which is scheduled to leave this evening at seven o'clock. Willie's engagements had called him from home in the early morning. Mrs. Chambers, Miss Effie, and Mr. Collom accompany Mrs. Shaw and myself to Oakland and take dinner with us in the "Lafayette"; they are warm in their praises of the comfort and luxury of our train and our enjoyable manner of traveling.

The hour of departure is drawing near and the many friends we have made are gathered around to see us off. Mrs. T. E. Gaither, a former Pennsylvanian, now a resident of Oakland, presents each one of the tourists with a bouquet of fine roses gathered from her splendid, spacious lawn of ever-blooming sweetness. The inevitable "All aboard" is shouted, the last hand shake is given, and our train leaves behind another garden spot of grandeur.

So far as present indications point, our people have all made good use of their time and thoroughly enjoyed themselves. The kind brothers of Golden Gate and El Capitan Divisions and the many good people of Oakland and San Francisco who contributed so much toward our pleasure are at the present time subjects of the warmest praise and most flattering comments, as incidents connected with our visit are being talked over and discussed. I hear Brother Springer telling in a pleasing and animated manner of a visit he and some others made to the palatial residence and grounds of Lucius Booth, Esq. "Mr. Booth gave us," says Brother Springer, "the freedom of his magnificent lawn and park, that were beautified and adorned with all kinds, varieties, and colors of plants, fruits, and flowers. We were shown by Mr. Booth what he told us is the greatest curiosity to be found, located in his park, two strong natural springs, only eighteen inches apart; the flow of water from each is about equal. From one spring gurgles a stream of sulphur water, pungent to the smell and taste, with no indications of iron in its composition, while from the other flows a stream strongly impregnated with iron, but with no sign of a particle of sulphur in its ingredients. It is a puzzle to the scientific world, and naturalists pronounce it a 'marvelous freak of nature.'"

I hear many of our people speak in the highest terms of Brother R. L. Myers, secretary and treasurer of Golden Gate Division 364, who devoted himself so faithfully and earnestly to the interests of our party. Brothers Maxwell, Reagan, Waddington, and a number of others also speak in glowing terms of the courtesy shown them by members of the Board of Trade.

We leave Oakland at 7.40 Pacific time (10.40 Eastern), attached to a five-car train called the "Portland Flyer," which makes the trip from Oakland to Portland every five days. Engine 1793, in charge of Engineer J. Edwards, is drawing the train, which is conducted by D. H. McIntire; the brakemen are W. J. Mitchell and H. B. Stewart. A ride of 26 miles brings us to Port Costa, where the engine and ten cars are run on to the ferryboat "Salina" and transported across the strait of Carquicons to the old town of Benicia, at one time the capital of California.

The "Salina" is the largest ferryboat ever constructed, being 424 feet long, 116 feet wide, and 18 feet deep; its capacity is forty-four cars and an engine, regardless of size or weight. So smoothly does the "Salina" run that there is not a tremor, jar, or motion to tell you she is moving. Engine 1793 will run us to Davis, a distance of 77 miles.

It has grown dark, a matter we always regret, for we never get tired watching the fleeting, ever-varying landscape. With prospects of mountains for to-morrow, we seek our little bed.

## MONDAY, MAY 24th.

Arose early this morning while it was hardly yet light, not wishing to miss any of the grand scenery that I know we must be nearing. Very few of our people are up, and making my way to the smoker I find the conductor who is running the train. He is a newcomer, an entire stranger, but I find him a very agreeable gentleman. "Where are we, captain?" I inquire. "Well," he answers pleasantly, "you are on the famous Shasta Route of the Southern Pacific Railroad, bound from San Francisco, Cal., to Portland, Ore., a distance of 772 miles. You have traveled about 200 miles in your sleep. We left Red Bluff a short time ago and are now approaching Redding, 260 miles from San Francisco and over 500 from Portland." "Where did you take charge of our train, please, and what is the number of your engine and the names of your crew?" I ask; "I'm trying to keep a little record of things as we go along," I add by way of explanation, as he looks askance at me. "I took your train at Red Bluff; have engine 1769, Engineer J. Clark. I can't tell you the fireman's name; my name is G. E.

Morgan, and my brakemen are J. Cook and J. Duncan. We take you to Ashland, a run of 206 miles. It will be necessary for us to get a helper engine shortly, for we have uphill work through here."

"What stream of water is this, captain?" I ask, as I look out of the window and see a large surging, gurgling, dashing stream of water that seems to be rushing past at a mile a minute gait. "That is the Sacramento River, a stream whose course you ascend for 307 miles and cross eighteen times between Sacramento and Sisson," he answers, rising and leaving the car as the train slows up and stops at a station.

I follow, get off, and look around. On the right the leaping, tumultuous waters of the Sacramento throw spray in your face as you stand and watch them churning and foaming in resistless might as they sweep madly onward toward the bay; on the left is the station and town of Redding. Several of our people are up and out on the ground. We can see that the town is a thriving business-looking place, and the station is a neat, substantial building. Our engine is taking water and the men are loading the tender with wood. "Why do you burn wood instead of coal in your engines?" I ask Conductor Morgan, who is standing near. "For the sake of economy, I suppose," he replies. "Wood is plenty and cheap, while coal is very scarce and expensive."

As we continue on our way I am reminded of Conductor Morgan's assertion that "wood is plenty," for we see thousands of cords piled up along the railroad track ready for use or awaiting shipment, and all the hills and slopes and mountain sides within our range of vision are covered with immense forests of pine and spruce. It is wild, picturesque mountain scenery and we all enjoy it.

Our train stops again, and looking out we see a name above the little station door that makes us think of home. It is the beloved, familiar Chester county name of Kennet. We notice that it is spelled with only one "t," but it is "Kennett," all the same. Stepping off, I see them attaching a helper engine and get its number, 1902.

As we start again I step on board, and entering the smoker encounter Brakeman Cook. "I suppose we have some climbing to do," I remark; "I see you've got an extra engine." "Yes," he responds, "from here to Sisson is 61 miles, and in that distance we make an ascent of 2884 feet, at one point having a grade of 168 feet to the mile." Passing Castle Crag we see in the distance its bald, bare bluffs and peaks of rugged, towering granite, and nestling in the shadow of the ridge can be seen its picturesque hotel, a resort where those needing mountain air for health, or mountain solitude for repose or pleasure, can find a safe, secure retreat.

From this point we catch our first glimpse of grand Mt. Shasta, 60 miles away. We stop at Dunsmuir twenty minutes for our engines to renew their supply of wood and water, and several passengers from the "Portland Flyer," taking advantage of the delay, went into a nearby hotel and got lunch. A boy on the station platform with a large four-pound trout that he had just caught, and which was still flapping its tail, attracts the attention of Brothers Sloane and Haas, who want the train held four hours while they go fishing, but the proposition is voted down. A beautiful large lawn slopes from the Dunsmuir Hotel to the railroad, on which tame mountain deer are browsing. Three miles from Dunsmuir we reach Mossbrae Falls and Shasta Soda Springs. Our train stops, and with cups, mugs, jugs, bottles, buckets, and pitchers we make a break for the fountain. There is plenty of water there, and oh, how cold and sparkling and invigorating it is! We drink our fill and fill our vessels and load the train, but it would not be missed had we taken ten thousand times as much. A roofed and stone-walled well that is inexhaustible is fed by hundreds of little streams and rivulets and jets that flow and spurt from the moss-covered mountain side, while here and there a spring more powerful than the rest sends its slender column full fifty feet in the air and then descends in a shower of mist around you.

Where is the artist that can picture the beauty of Mossbrae Falls, a mighty mountain side covered to its summit with giant pines, terminating at its base in a sheer wall a hundred feet in height, its face covered and festooned with bright green moss, through which descends in a silvery sheen of spray the outpour from a thousand gushing springs? From here to Sisson, a distance of 25 miles, our engines have trying uphill work. There are mountains everywhere, mountains ahead of us and mountains behind us, mountains above us and mountains below us, mountains to the right and mountains to the left, but they are not the bald, bare, treeless kind, for everywhere you look, except when you cast your eye to Shasta's crown, you will see a magnificent growth of pines and cedars, shrubbery and ferns. You have always to look up or else look down. Looking up you can scarcely ever see the pine-clad summits, for your eye rests on the top of the car window before it reaches half way up the mountain side; looking down you are all right, if you don't get dizzy, for in many places you can look down upon the tops of the tallest trees a thousand feet below.

With breath of flame and lungs of iron those powerful iron steeds puff and cough and climb, and the long ten-car train, following their laborious lead, winds and worms in and out and around those narrow paths, traced and hewn in the mighty Sierra Nevada's rugged sides by persistent resistless Progress, ever guided, ever urged by the indomitable will, restless perseverance, mechanical ingenuity, and scientific skill of man. We climb and climb and worm and wind until Sisson's heights are reached, at an elevation of 3555 feet, and then we rest awhile—rest to feast our eyes on Shasta's indescribable majesty and grandeur.

This is the nearest point the railroad runs to that gigantic mound, and it is twelve miles on an air line from where we sit and stand to the glistening, snow-crowned crest of that mighty monarch. Why we should so sensibly feel his presence and he so far away is a conundrum no one asks; we only look and feel, and silently wonder what it is we feel. It must be awe, for that which is great, we are told, inspires awe, and Shasta is very, very great. Fourteen thousand four hundred and forty-two feet is the estimated height of this colossal giant that pokes his apex in the sky. Were it possible to grade him down or slice him off to one-half his height he would make a plateau 75 miles in circumference and 25 miles across; but it is time to go. The manager says, "Git on," and bidding adieu to Shasta we "git."

One mile from Sisson Conductor Morgan points to a

little mountain spring that wouldn't slake the thirst of a nanny goat, and says, "There's the head waters of the Sacramento River, which is 307 miles from where it empties into the bay." The road now is making some wonderful curves and bends to get around insurmountable heights and across unbridgeable chasms. We have just finished a run of about eight miles, described almost a complete S, and are only one mile and a half from where we started. At Edgewood helper engine No. 1902 is detached, for it is now down grade to Hornbrook, a distance of 40 miles, with a drop at places of 170 feet to the mile.

At Hornbrook engine No. 1907 was attached to assist to Siskiyou, a distance of 24 miles, with an ascent of 190 feet to the mile. As we approach State Line we cross the old Portland stage trail, and at 3.03 P. M. Eastern (12.03 Pacific) time we cross the State Line and enter Oregon, having traveled 1136 miles through the State of California. We pass Gregory Siding, where two freight wrecks had recently occurred. The wrecking crew are still on the ground, having evidently just put engine No. 1503 on the track, for it is standing there as we pass, covered with mud. We here have in view Pilot Rock, a great bare bluff that stands out and alone like a huge sentinel guarding the gateway of the valley, and famous in the early history of this locality as the scene of stirring Indian warfare. Manager and Mrs. Wyman are on the engine enjoying an unobstructed view of this marvelous mountain ride. We have just had our last look at California scenery, for rounding a bend as we pass Pilot Rock, the last view of majestic Shasta bursts upon our vision, reposing in sublime and solemn grandeur 50

miles away. Another curve, the picture fades, the curtain falls, and exit California.

Still climbing the rugged sides of Siskiyou, and drawing nearer and closer to its summit, our train, as though despairing of ever reaching the top, plunges suddenly into its rocky ribs. The depths of despair can be no darker than the gloomy obscurity of this yawning hole in the mountain wall; for 3700 feet through "Tunnel 13" our train pierces the heart of Siskiyou before emerging into daylight on the opposite side. Here the summit of the grade is reached at an elevation of 4130 feet. Leaving engine No. 1907 behind we now commence the descent of the northern slope of the Siskiyou Mountain, amidst scenery of beauty and grandeur. Arriving at Ashland 5.10 P. M. Eastern (2.10 P. M. Pacific) time, a stop of twenty minutes is given and a change of engines is made.

Bidding goodbye to Conductor Morgan and his crew, who deserve our highest praise for the able manner in which our train was handled, and who did much toward making the trip interesting by the useful information imparted, we speed on our way again with engine 1361 in charge of C. C. Case and fired by Robert McCuan; Conductor Edward Houston, Baggagemaster R. W. Jameson, Brakeman H. Ballard, who take us to Portland, 341 miles. Leaving Ashland, we pass a number of gold mines in operation on the rugged hillside, and swing around into Rogue River Valley, a rich farming and fruit-growing district, producing, it is said, some of the finest fruits grown in Oregon. A stop of a few minutes is made at Grant's Pass, attaching engine No. 1759 to assist up the hill to West Fork, 47 miles.

Twenty minutes is allowed at Glendale to enable the passengers of the "Portland Flyer" and the crew to partake of lunch at "The Hotel Glendale." Soon after leaving Glendale we enter a wild ravine, inclosed by towering hills covered to their summits with great pine timber. "Mr. Jameson," I ask of the baggagemaster, an agreeable old gentleman, "has this wild spot a name?" "This is Cow Creek Cañon; the stream of water you see is Cow Creek, which runs the entire length of the cañon, 35 miles," is the answer.

The farther we penetrate this narrow gorge the more are we impressed with the solitude of its mighty pine-clad sides, that commence at the creek on one hand and at the railroad on the other and rise upward in a steep slope for over 2000 feet, covered to the very crests with giant Oregon pines. We arrive at the little station of West Fork, the only station in the cañon, and engine No. 1759 is detached and sidetracked. There is gold hidden in these mighty hils, and here and there we see a mine, the principal one, the Victoria, being located near West Fork. Two miles north of this point we are shown where occurred in 1890 the largest landslide ever known in the history of railroads. An immense section of the mountain side becoming loosened, slid down into the bottom of the cañon, burying 900 feet of the railroad to the depth of 100 feet, and damming the creek, formed a lake 60 feet deep and one mile long. The buried track was abandoned and the road built across the creek along the foot of the opposite sloping wall of the cañon. We can plainly see the great mass of earth and rocks and trees that cover the buried track, and which forms a striking instance of what might occur at any time to roads that run through such mountain cañons. It is growing dark as we emerge from the fastness and solitude of this Oregon wilderness, but can easily discern that it is a change for the better, for we enter a valley teeming with fields of waving grain and orchards of thrifty trees. We stop at Roseburg for ten minutes, where another change of engines is made, and when we start on our way again at 12.10 A. M. Eastern (9.10 P. M. Pacific) time, it is quite dark.

Leaving Roseburg, we have engine No. 1355, with Engineer Montgomery at the throttle. Having a grade for 15 miles between Drains and Cottage Grove, we get Engineer Connelly, with engine No. 1516, as helper. Conductor Houston and his crew continue with us to Portland.

## TUESDAY, MAY 25th.

Arrived at Portland this morning at 8.00 Eastern (5.00 Pacific) time, and after breakfast we met Morton Young, Esq., of Portland. Mr. Young is a member of Mt. Hood Division No. 91, O. R. C., and an earnest and enthusiastic member of the order, though not in railway service at the present time, having been fortunate in real estate speculation and able now to retire from active business cares. Brother Young kindly escorts a number of our party over the East Side Electric Railway to Oregon City, which is a pleasant ride of 14 miles. We climb the great wooden stairway leading up to the bluffs that overlook the city and obtain a magnificent view of all the surrounding country. Looking down upon the falls of the Willamette River, we are impressed with the grandeur of this Niagara of the Pacific. Descending from this alluring point of observation, we visit the great electric plant located at the falls, deriving its power from the waters of the Willamette and supplying Oregon City, Portland, and all the outlying districts with light and power. From the windows of the power house we obtain a much nearer view of the falls. The Willamette River at this point is about half a mile in width and the falls, in the form of a semi-circle, extend from shore to shore with an average height of 40 feet. It is estimated that the horse-power capacity of this great volume of leaping, dashing, roaring water is second in the world to that of Niagara. The great power house, with walls of solid concrete, is located on the west side of the river, just below the falls, and has a capacity of 12,000 horse power. It is owned and operated by the Portland General Electric Company, a corporation organized in 1892 with a capital of $4,250,000.

We cannot remain long in one place and are unable to give this interesting city the attention we would like, but we can see as we traverse one of its principal thoroughfares that it is up to date in its accommodations and improvements. We pass the Electric Hotel, and from its appearance we are sure it is first class in every respect, and had we the opportunity or occasion to partake of its hospitality we are confident we would be well taken care of by the proprietors who manage the establishment, Mr. and Mrs. W. M. Robinson. We visit the fish market and are interested in the salmon just brought in, that range in weight from five to fifty pounds, the streams through this part of the country abounding with this species of fish. The ladies, intent on pro-

THE COLUMBIA RIVER.

curing souvenirs, visit a number of the stores as we go along. On the river banks are located numerous mills and factories. Arriving at the point where we take the electric line for Portland and finding a car waiting, we get aboard and start again on the delightful 14-mile trolley ride. Among the passengers in the car is a lady whose pleasant countenance invites confidence, and Mrs. Shaw has entered into conversation with her. I am busy looking off across the country, enjoying the beauty of the landscape, and have given their talk no attention. Brother Young has just pointed out Clackamas Heights and is now trying to show us the snow crown of Mt. Hood, but his Honor is so mixed up with the vapory clouds that hang around the horizon that he cannot be located. A nudge from Mrs. S. invites my attention, and as I turn she introduces her new-found friend, Mrs. Robinson, of the Electric Hotel, Oregon City. Mrs. Robinson is a bright conversationalist and entertained us with some facts about the city and its surroundings.

"Do you like Oregon City?" some one asks. "I not only like it," answers Mrs. Robinson, "but I am proud of it. It is a town with a history. The site of Oregon City was first located in the year 1829 by Dr. John McLoughlin, an agent of the Hudson Bay Company, who established a trading post here. It was here a few years later that the Methodists built the first Protestant church erected on the Pacific slope. The Oregon *Spectator*, the first newspaper published on the Pacific coast, was printed here in 1846 on a press brought from the Sandwich Islands. We have a climate," she continued, "that never goes to extremes;

we seldom have freezing weather, and snow, if it comes, only lasts a few hours. I have gathered roses in my yard on Christmas, for very rarely the cold is severe enough to destroy our flowers. We have not grown so rapidly as some of the younger cities of the Northwest, but we have all the natural advantages and facilities to insure and encourage progress and development. We have excellent graded schools that are well attended, and as an evidence of the educational importance of our city, the Willamette Valley Chautauqua Association holds its annual convention or assembly at Gladstone Park, not far from Oregon City. These meetings are largely attended, thousands coming from all parts of the Pacific coast. The people will commence to gather for these meetings next week, and I expect we will have our hands full; but here's where I get off," and rising as the car stops she bids us goodday and steps off.

We have reached Portland, and after proceeding a few blocks under the guidance of Brother Young, we leave the electric road and board a cable car for Portland Heights, a high eminence overlooking the city and commanding a magnificent view of all the surrounding country for many miles. We gaze down upon three rivers, the Columbia, Willamette, and Clackamas, and follow with our eyes their sinuous windings as their waters gleam and glimmer in the sun. We can plainly see the hoary crests of Mt. Adams and Saint Helens, but clouds still hovering on the eastern horizon keep Mt. Hood hidden from our sight. With the perversity of human nature, that is always hankering for what is beyond its reach, we want a look at Mt. Hood. "We came up here to see it," says Mrs. Dougherty, "and if

J. P. O'BRIEN, SUPERINTENDENT RAIL LINES, OREGON RAILROAD AND NAVIGATION COMPANY.

it's only a wee glimpse I want it." So do we all, and we keep our gaze riveted on the spot where Brother Young says it will appear, if it shows at all.

"Mt. Hood is 70 miles away," says Brother Young, "but on a perfectly clear day a person from here can see it very plainly." The clouds showing no inclination to favor us, we descend from the Heights, get aboard a car, and start for the station, where we arrive about 1.30 P. M., and find the most of our people gathered there; they also have spent a very pleasant morning taking in the sights of Portland and gathering souvenirs.

Brothers Maxwell and Reagan, of the excursion executive committee, have not been idle, but calling upon Superintendent J. P. O'Brien, of the Oregon River and Navigation Company Rail Lines, have arranged for an excursion this afternoon up the banks of the Columbia River to Cascade Locks and return.

Getting lunch at a near-by restaurant, we are soon all ready for the start. Our three sleepers are attached to a regular train that leaves at 2.45 P. M. "Are all our people here?" asks Manager Wyman, surveying the crowd. "There are four or five that are absent, I believe," answers Secretary Maxwell, as he nips the northeast corner off a plug of tobacco. "Sloane and Haas are not here, I know," speaks out Brother Terry, "for they went out with a boy in a boat to watch the salmon shoot the falls of the Willamette and haven't got back yet." "Time's up; can't wait; all aboard," shouts the conductor, and away we go, bound for a trip of 45 miles through the marvelous and unsurpassed scenery of the Columbia River. Superintendent O'Brien is with us, his private car being attached to the train. Chief Dispatcher E. N. Campbell, C. R. Holcomb, Esq., and Brother M. Young also accompany the party. L. J. Hicks, photographer, of Portland, is along in his professional capacity; we are also accompanied by the Portland Hotel orchestra, comprised of the following gentlemen: G. H. Parsons, J. Seltenraick, F. Boyd, William Livinston, Prof. E. F. Fleck, who render admirable and pleasing music. Many are the expressions of delight as we catch fleeting glimpses of the wonderful scenery. "You will have a better view on the return trip," advises Mr. O'Brien, "for we will then run slow and make an occasional stop." Arriving at Cascade Locks, we are given twenty minutes to visit the great locks which the Government is about completing, at a cost of nearly $1,500,000, to enable vessels to reach the highest navigable point of this most remarkable river.

Time is up to start on our return trip, and reaching the train we find O. R. & N. engine No. 73 coupled to the train, with Engineer A. Curtis and Fireman Jo. Wilson in the cab and Conductor J. A. Allison standing near ready to move off as soon as we are ready to go. In a minute we are all on, and the train goes slowly down the great Columbia, whose current, always rapid, is augmented and increased twofold by the melting snows in the mountains, and surges past in an angry, turbid torrent. From the rushing waters of the mighty river on one side we look up on the other side to the towering cliffs and crags and peaks that rise in majesty and grandeur 3000 feet in the air, their summits fringed with pines that look like ferns as they wave against the sky, while here and there, from out those walls of rock, mountain streams gush forth, and falling hundreds of

MT. ADAMS, WASHINGTON.

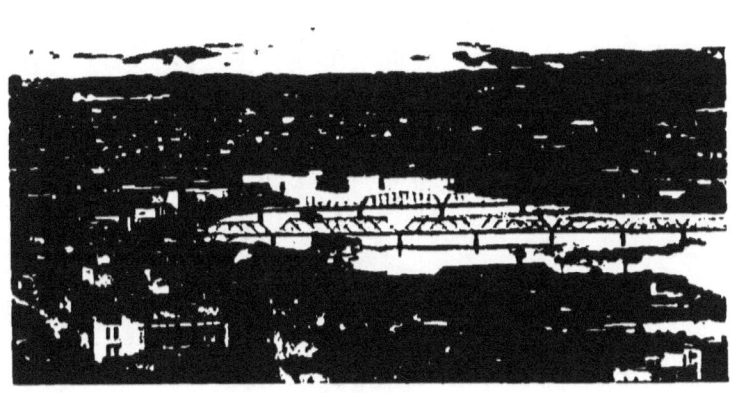

MT. ST. HELENS, FROM PORTLAND.

feet, their waters descend in showers of rainbow-tinted spray.

"Well," remarks Mr. O'Brien, as he sees we are almost speechless with rapture and delight, "that's something you don't see in Pennsylvania or Jersey every day in the year." "No," I respond, "nor anywhere else in the world on any day of the year." "I really believe there is no scenery in the whole wide world more intensely absorbing than your Columbia River scenery, Mr. O'Brien," says Mrs. Mattson, and the Doctor, standing near, smiles down upon her his approval. "We will now turn our attention to something more practical than towering mountains and leaping waterfalls," says Mr. O'Brien, as the train comes to a stop. "We will show you how our salmon are coaxed out of the water."

Leading the way, we follow him down the river bank to its edge and on to a platform or wharf extending for several feet into the water, where a large wheel is slowly revolving that looks something like the side wheel of an old-fashioned ferryboat or the large overshot water wheel of an old-time sawmill, except that it turns backward, and as the scoops or buckets rise out of the water they bring the fish along, should any of them be so unfortunate as to get caught. When the scoop rises to a certain height the fish slip out into an incline trough or chute (something like the "boys" had fun with at Sutro's) and are dumped into a bin under the platform. "We are not catching many at the present time," says the man who is operating the trap, "the river is too high and muddy and the fish are not running very lively." Opening a trap door, he allows us to peer down into the bin, where we see a lot of fish of various sizes. He kindly gave us several for our dining car, an act we all highly appreciate.

We next stop at Multnomah Falls, where one of those mountain streams pouring over the face of a cliff has a sheer descent of 950 feet. Here the party is arranged in a group on a grassy slope, with the falls as background, and photographed by Mr. Hicks. "Mr. Hicks, will all those beautiful rainbows we see there show in the pictures you have taken?" asks Mrs. Matthews of the photographer. "No," replies Mr. Hicks, "that is beyond our art. No camera will picture nor can artist paint the gorgeous coloring and beautifully blended tints that you see in the dashing spray of Multnomah Falls." "I don't know about that," answers Brother Mart. Houston, who is always of a practical turn of mind. "I believe George Cope, of Chester County, could do it, for a man who can paint the pretty spots of a trout or all the colors of autumnal foliage and never miss a tint can come pretty close to Multnomah Falls." "He ought to come out here and paint it, then," responds Brother Bob Foulon; "for a reproduction of Multnomah Falls on canvas as we see it to-day could not be surpassed by any painting in the world." We all echo Brother Foulon's sentiments, and feel as we get aboard the train that it has been our privilege to look upon a scene of unequaled loveliness and grandeur.

We again stop and are photographed at the Pillar, an enormous column of rock standing alone between the river and the railroad, upon the summit of which is growing a great pine tree, 1000 feet in the air. We get back to the depot about 7.30 and find McDonald has a sumptuous dinner awaiting us, which we all

MULTNOMAH FALLS, OREGON.

heartily enjoy. Mr. O'Brien and Brother Young take dinner with us, and our people show their appreciation of the courtesy and kindness of these gentlemen by giving them three rousing cheers. After supper Manager E. Lyons, of the Union Depot, escorts a number of the "boys" to the luxurious quarters of the Commercial Club, where we are royally entertained for three hours, returning to the train about midnight.

## WEDNESDAY, MAY 26th.

Everybody is astir in good time this morning, for we are soon to bid adieu to this great city of the far Northwest, where we have been so kindly treated and royally entertained. The warmhearted brothers of Mt. Hood Division No. 91, O. R. C., along with the officers of the different transportation companies, will long be remembered for their generous manner toward us. "Views of Portland, Oregon, and the Columbia River," a beautiful pamphlet souvenir issued by Mt. Hood Division, was presented to each member of our party, and is highly prized. In connection with the pamphlet is "a ticket of welcome" of coupon form, and is quite lengthy, but all right, the first clause of which reads, "This contract with coupons attached entitles the holder to a hearty welcome and a first-class reception on entering the State of Oregon, and the courtesies of the Southern Pacific Company, the Oregon Railroad and Navigation Company, and the Northern Pacific Railway.

R. KOEHLER,
General Manager S. P.

E. MCNEILL,
Pres. & Mgr. O. R. & N.

W. H. HULBURT,
G. P. A., O. R. & N. Co.

J. H. HANNAFORD,
Genl. Traffic Mgr. N. P. Ry.

E. P. ROGERS,
A. G. P. A., S. P.

B. CAMPBELL,
Traffic Mgr. O. R. & N.

J. W. KENDRICK,
Genl. Mgr. N. P. Ry.

C. S. FEE,
G. P. A., N. P. Ry."

There are five clauses in the contract. The last clause reads, "The Reception Committee will not be responsible for the loss of any diamonds (kings and queens excepted), baggage, meals, or sleep on this run.

J. M. POORMAN,      J. W. CROCKER,
Sec. & Treas.            C. C.

"MT. HOOD DIVISION No. 91, O. R. C."

There are six coupons, each reading to and fro over a line between different points of interest, and bearing at the bottom the name of the superintendent over whose line it reads. The whole is a nicely gotten up affair and a valued addition to our collection of souvenirs.

We leave here at 8.45 A. M., and the hour of departure being at hand (as is always the case), a number of our new-found friends are at hand to see us off. All along our route we have been constantly reminding the people who we are by a yell we give in concert, with a vim that would drown the racket of a college football team; and now, gathered in a bunch, we let go:—

"Who are we? O. R. C.

"Pennsylvania employé.

"Rah! rah! boom—ah!"

The ladies of our party are ready and let go:—

"Who are we? Who are we?

"The wives and the daughters of the O. R. C.

"Rah! rah! boom—ah!"

And now the cooks and waiters gathered at the windows and on the platform of the "Lafayette" let go:—

"Who are we? P. P. C.

ALONG THE COLUMBIA RIVER.

"The cooks and the waiters of the O. R. C.
"Rah! rah! boom—ah!"
With all this din ringing in their ears the good people of Portland see our train pulling away from their beautiful station. As they wave their adieus we pass from their sight on a run of 146 miles over the Northern Pacific Railway to Tacoma, Wash. N. P. engine No. 617 is drawing us, managed by Engineer F. W. Bockerman and fired by H. Deam. The conductor is Henry Buckley and the brakemen are H. Harkins and Tom Martin; Mr. Martin is a young man from Chester County, Pennsylvania, who has come West to seek his fortune, and has accepted the position of a brakeman with the expectation of rising in the ranks, and we wish him success.

From Portland to Goble, 39 miles, we follow the Columbia River, which is very high, and much of the low land is submerged. We can see buildings surrounded by water that have been vacated, and we are reminded of the El Paso flood. We look beyond this desolating waste of water and in the far distance can see the glistening summits of Mt. Hood and Saint Helens. Reaching Goble, our train is run on to the great ferry steamer "Tacoma," transported across the Columbia River to Kalama, and into the State of Washington. Leaving Kalama, we pass through a fine farming country, where agricultural industries seem to be extensively carried on. After passing Centralia, which is a flourishing town of about 3000 inhabitants, we have a splendid view of Mt. Rainier for several miles while we sweep across the Yelm prairie. A short stop is made at Roy to pick up Brothers B. W. Johnson and

S. H. Ewalt, of Mt. Tacoma Division No. 249, O. R. C., who are members of committee on entertainment, and who promise to show us the city of Tacoma after our arrival there. The country through here seems to be rich in natural resources, for bordering the fertile valleys can be seen heavily timbered hills and here and there a coal mine in operation.

Arriving in Tacoma at 4.40 P. M. Eastern (1.40 P. M. Pacific), we are immediately taken out by Brothers Johnson and Ewalt to see the town and are joined by A. F. Haines, passenger agent of Northern Pacific Railway, Capt. A. Thompson, of the Portland *Oregonian*, C. P. Ferry, Esq. (who bears the distinguished title of "Duke of Tacoma"), and a member of the Chamber of Commerce, L. Ceasar, Esq., president of Tacoma Bank and a member of the Board of Trade. The first place we visit is the County Court House. "This," says Mr. Ferry, "is one of the finest buildings in Tacoma, which, you know, is the county seat of Pierce County. We had to have a court house and thought we would build a good one; it cost $400,000." We amused ourselves looking through the museum located in this building, many of the relics and works of art having been contributed by Mr. Ferry, who collected many of them in foreign countries through which he has traveled. We spent half an hour in the Court House and then entered into a street car, which took us a much-enjoyed ride through the city to Point Defiance Park.

To form a true conception of a Washington forest one has but to visit this wonderful park. Such majestic trees we never saw before, many of them six and eight feet in diameter and estimated to be 300 feet in height, great

C STREET, TACOMA, WASHINGTON.

BRIDGE, POINT DEFIANCE PARK, TACOMA, WASHINGTON.

pines and cedars, natural growth of the soil, and amongst them, growing in wild profusion, great ferns six feet in height. In inclosures can be seen deer, elk, and bear, natives of the wilds. Through this great forest park bridle paths lead in all directions, and about 80 miles of bicycle track is built. The park is situated on a high eminence overlooking Puget Sound. By a series of steep paths and stairs we descend to the beach. The sound is a great body of water with hardly a ripple on its surface. A half hour is spent here gathering pebbles and shells, and then we head for the smelter, half a mile up the beach.

A boathouse furnishes rowboats for those who want them, and a number avail themselves of this opportunity to avoid a tiresome walk. Those who walk ascend again the steps and steep pathway, and going along the forest walk they arrive at the smelter the same time as those who rowed. We are taken through the great hot, smoky building and shown the treatment ore receives in all its stages from the smelter to the crucible. This immense plant, owned and operated by the Tacoma Smelting and Refining Company, handles gold, silver, and copper ore, and has an annual output of over $900,000. A train of cars await us when we emerge from the works, flat cars, fitted up with seats for the occasion; upon these we climb, and find as we are slowly taken along the sound front that no conveyance could afford a better view. Tacoma has 12 miles of a water front, upon which splendid wharves, great warehouses, monster elevators, immense saw and flour mills are built, the whole 12 miles being lined with industries of this character.

This trip over, we return to our train and find dinner

awaiting us, after which our train is run to the steamboat landing and we are taken aboard the "City of Kingston," belonging to the Northern Pacific Railway, for a trip of 28 miles to Seattle. We can hardly realize as the boat leaves the wharf that our visit to Tacoma is over, so rapidly were we hustled along; but we are highly pleased with the treatment we received and feel that Tacoma is a wonderful place and her people will make her still more wonderful by their thrift, their push, and activity. They have our best wishes for their future progress and advancement.

The "City of Kingston" is a splendid boat and rides like a feather over the waters of the sound, and from the expressions of delight on every hand it is evident our people are enjoying the trip. The boat is in charge of Engineer G. H. Lent and a gentlemanly purser, who have won the goodwill of our party by kindly allowing us the freedom of the boat and showing us through many of the elegantly-furnished state rooms with which the boat is equipped. Arriving at Seattle, we are loaded in a large cable car and taken through the city for about four miles and back again. It is so dark we cannot see the town and can only enjoy the ride. We are taken to the station, where we wait for half an hour for our train to arrive, which has been sent from Tacoma to overtake us. We are all pretty thoroughly tired out, and are glad when at about eleven o'clock our train arrives, and we are soon making ourselves comfortable inside. M. M. Davis, Esq., a press representative of Seattle, and Conductor Thomas Doyle in search of an "item" gave us a short call just after our train came over from Tacoma. Brother Reagan and "Alfalfa" are the only ones I see as

LATOURELLE FALLS, OREGON.

I leave the "refreshment corner" in the "combined" to seek repose in the "Marco." Our train is still standing at Seattle and the hour is close to midnight.

## THURSDAY, MAY 27th.

Getting up this morning about 7.30, I find we are crossing another desert—at least it has that appearance. We have left Ellensburg and are running through a dry, sandy country along the Yakima River. Here and there we pass a ranch where plots of land under irrigation are being cultivated, and from the fertile appearance of these irrigated tracts it would seem that this country needs but plenty of water to make it a blooming paradise. This much I discover by looking out the window while waiting my turn to wash and comb, for Brothers Terry, Brown, and Horner are ahead of me this morning. We work on the principle "first come first served," and all good naturedly wait when there is nothing else to do. Completing my toilet, I go to the smoker and find the genial conductor who is running the train, and learn that he is a member of Mt. Hood Division No. 91; name, W. B. Hale.

"I took charge of your train at Ellensburg," he says, on being asked the question, "and am going with you as far as I can. We have engine No. 333, run by Engineer Brant, who will take us to Pasco, 122 miles." "This is a barren-looking country for stock raising," I remark, as I see a large drove of cattle kicking up the dust in the desert as we pass them; "what do they live on?" "Those cattle are from away back toward the hills, where there is plenty of 'bunch grass' that they feed on, and are coming to the irrigation canal for water, or perhaps they are being driven to the railroad station for shipment. You would be surprised at the amount of stock shipped from North Yakima, Prosser, and Kennewick," is the reply. "There seems to be no trouble about growing plenty of stuff where there is water," I venture to assert, seeing a verdant-looking plantation, like an oasis in the desert, a short distance away. "Lack or scarcity of water is the only hindrance to agricultural industry," is the answer, "and this drawback is being rapidly overcome by the construction of large irrigating canals by companies formed for that purpose."

"Breakfast is now ready in the dining car," chimes the welcome voice of Conductor McDonald at the open door. Several of our people had entered the smoker during the last half hour, and all arise as one person at the music of that well-known voice, that always brings "tidings of great joy." "I think Mr. McDonald has the loveliest voice, for a man," is the flattering remark of Mrs. Matthews as we make a break for the diner. Not one of us but what thinks so too, but of course we know Mrs. Matthews is thinking of the song McDonald sang to us a few evenings before.

"There's a tramp hidden between the ice chests under this car beating his way, I heard some one say awhile ago," says Manager Wyman at the breakfast table. As we finish eating the train stops at the little station of Kiona and we all get out to see the stowaway. Sure enough he's there. In a narrow space between the ice chests, about 16 inches wide, he has placed a board on the dining-car ladder which is kept there, and crawled in on it, a place so narrow that he cannot change his posi-

THE HOBO PASSENGER.

CROSSING COLUMBIA RIVER ON THE "TACOMA."

tion or turn. We can see him all covered with dust, but he does not move, and we are not sure that he is alive, for this Yakima dust is something terrible and he has certainly got a dose of it. One of the dining-car boys brought him out some bread and meat, a can of water, and a sponge to protect his mouth and nostrils from the dust. We can see that he is alive when these things are pushed into him, for he reaches out a hand as far as he can to receive them. After passing Kennewick we cross the Columbia River and are soon at Pasco, where a stop is made to change engines. While this is being done we persuade our "mascot" to come from beneath the car. As he crawls from his hiding place and straightens up Brother Ristein, who has his kodak ready, takes a snap. We can see through the ginger-colored Yakima dust on his face that he is a negro. "What's your name?" I ask. "John Bell, sah." "Where do you live?" asks Brother Matthews.. "Al'bama, sah." "Where did you get on this car?" asks Manager Wyman. "Tacoma, sah." "How did you get to Tacoma?" asks Brother Dougherty. "Cargo hosses, sah." "Where do you want to go, now?" asks Conductor Hale. "Montana, sah." "Well, crawl in your hole; we're going to start," replies Captain Hale, and turning to Manager Wyman continues, "We may as well allow him to keep his place, for soon as you rout him out there will be another one ready to crawl in. It's impossible to get through this part of the country without being troubled with hoboes."

We leave Pasco at 12.55 Eastern (9.45 Pacific) time with engine No. 405, Engineer Tom Allen and Fireman W. W. Thompson, who run us to Spokane, 146 miles. Much of the country through which we are now passing is very dry and barren-looking, but we are informed by Captain Hale that it is considered a rich grazing district. From Lind to Sprague, a distance of 45 miles, many large herds of horses and cattle are seen. Just before reaching Sprague we run for two miles on the border of Spring Lake, a fine body of water that looks very refreshing after so many miles of dry and dusty territory. We stop at Sprague a few minutes for water and notice the place has had a very serious fire not long since.

"Captain," I ask, addressing Brother Hale, who is near by, "what has happened to Sprague?" "The town was nearly wiped out about a year ago by a very bad fire," is the reply, "and it is a great pity, for Sprague was a pretty little place and a thriving town. It is the county seat of Lincoln County, and had a population of about 2000. It is the headquarters of the Idaho Division of the Northern Pacific Railway, and the company's machine shops and roundhouse were completely destroyed and all those engines ruined," and he points to where can be seen about a dozen locomotives, burned and warped, standing on the tracks that had been the interior of the roundhouse and shops.

Another run of 25 miles through good farming and grazing territory, interspersed with considerable timber land, brings us to Cheney, where we again make a short stop. Since crossing the Columbia our course has been upward, and from an elevation at Kennewick of 350 feet we have now reached 2300 feet. Cheney is a growing business place of 1200 inhabitants. It is nicely located on the great plateau of the Columbia and surrounded for many miles with rich farm land and abundant timber.

ELEVATOR A, TACOMA, WASHINGTON

SHORE OF LAKE PEND D'OREILLE AT HOPE, IDAHO.

Here we meet Mr. H. W. McMaster, chief dispatcher of Northern Pacific Railway at Spokane, whom we find to be a very courteous and agreeable gentleman. On a sidetrack near where our train stands, Mr. McMaster shows us the largest locomotive on the Northern Pacific Railway, No. 150. Engine and tender without fuel or water weigh 106 tons; it has a 34-inch cylinder; was built in Schenectady, N. Y., since the first of the year. They have had it but a short time but find it very satisfactory. It is in charge of Engineer J. Bruce and is run in the freight service between Spokane and Pasco. Mr. McMaster accompanies us to Spokane, where we arrive at 5.20 P. M. Eastern (2.20 P. M. Pacific), and are met at the station by Dr. E. D. Olmsted, Mayor of Spokane. We are introduced to the Mayor by Mr. McMaster in a neat little speech. His Honor responds in a pleasant manner, bidding us welcome and giving us the freedom of the city. The street railway management offers us the use and freedom of their lines so long as we wish to remain in the city. We have but two hours here, and the municipal authorities and street railway managers vie with one another in their efforts to show us as much of the city as possible in the short time we will be with them. A number of carriages are sent around and quickly loaded up, accommodating about one-half of the party, the remainder board street cars, and we start on a tour of the city.

Spokane is the county seat of Spokane County, with a population of about 32,000. It occupies a remarkably picturesque location on both sides of the Spokane River, a mighty mountain torrent, the rush and roar of whose eternal, resistless energy holds the visitors to-day spellbound and speechless with admiration, amazement, and awe. We had looked upon, we supposed, during the past two weeks, all varieties and degrees of running, rushing, and falling waters, but at no time have we gazed upon such a tumbling, seething, foaming, roaring torrent as this that now fascinates us with its sublime grandeur and astounds us with its terrific force.

Right through the centre of the city, with a fall of 150 feet in the space of half a mile, this mighty torrent tears, dashing and splashing, surging and foaming against and amongst the great rocks and boulders that beset its course with a fury that is indescribable, and we feel as we gaze upon this wonderful, awe-inspiring spectacle that there is no more limit to the power of the elements than there is to the measure of eternity. This magnificent river that never freezes runs the great electric plant that lights the city and operates 45 miles of electric railway. It furnishes power for numerous flour and saw mills, factories and foundries that can be seen in operation along its banks, giving an aspect of business activity to the place that is a pleasing manifestation of prosperity and enterprise.

Its fine, substantial, costly church, school, municipal, and other public buildings and superb private residences are indications that there is wealth in Spokane. Because of the advantages and facilities of its admirable location, surrounded by vast forests of valuable timber, fertile agricultural valleys, rich mining districts, and the traffic of seven railroads, we predict for Spokane a phenomenal future. It is destined, we are sure, at an early day to be the first city of the great Northwest. Not one of the party will ever forget our short visit to

SPOKANE FALLS, SPOKANE.

SPOKANE, WASHINGTON.

Spokane. Mr. McMaster took Brothers Maxwell and Reagan around with his own team and Captain Hale took Manager Wyman. The street-car party was under the escort of James Mendenhall, Esq., an old schoolmate of Brother James Matthews. Mr. Mendenhall came West several years ago, located at Spokane, and engaged in real estate business. He is now one of the prominent citizens of the place and closely identified with the business interests and enterprises of the city. We also met Mark Mendenhall, Esq., a brother of James, who is a leading attorney in Spokane. No, we will not forget the courtesy and kindness of the good people of Spokane, and the good people of Spokane will not forget us, for they have only to remember that on the afternoon of May 27th, 1897, street-railway traffic was blocked for thirty minutes by a car abandoned by the Pennsylvania Railroad conductors and kept waiting for them while they viewed the grandeur of Spokane Falls for half an hour from the rear balcony of the brewery.

At 7.40 P. M. Eastern (4.40 P. M. Pacific) time we are all aboard our train once more, and with Engineer Secord at the throttle of engine No. 119 we quickly leave beautiful Spokane far in our rear. Captain Hale is still with us, his brakeman being A. S. Harding. A hobo is discovered lying on the truss rods of the combined car; he can be seen by looking around the side of the car; his position seems a perilous one, but our train makes no stop till it gets to Hope, 84 miles, so he is allowed to remain and take his chances. For several miles we pass through magnificent cattle ranges and fine farming lands. As we approach Hope the road skirts the shores of Lake Pend d'Oreille for about three miles, giving us a fine view of this beautiful body of water. We arrive at Hope 10.00 Eastern (7.00 Pacific) time and stop twenty-five minutes to change engines. Here a change is also made in time; it changes from Pacific to Mountain time, one hour later than Pacific and two hours earlier than Eastern time. Hobo No. 2 changed his position from the truss rods of the combined car to a pile of ties when the train stopped at Hope. He was given a lunch by one of the dining-car boys and advised not to anchor himself in the same place again, as the position was not only a dangerous one, but very conspicuous. When asked his name he said it was J. W. Kelsey, that he was trying to get home, had been away for two years, and wanted to see his mother. Hobo No. 1 lays low, for he knows should he for a moment vacate his narrow quarters under the "Lafayette" there would be a scramble for his place. It is growing dusk, and through the gloom of the dying day we have counted no less than fifteen skulking forms about the train, watching for an opportunity to secrete themselves underneath or about the train for the purpose of obtaining free transportation.

Bidding adieu to big-hearted, genial Captain Hale, who has been with us for 357 miles, we leave Hope at 10.25 P. M. Eastern (8.25 P. M. Mountain) time with N. P. engine No. 438, with Engineer Jim Bailey at the throttle, whose fireman is John Ryan. Conductor William Gilbert has charge of the train and his brakemen are T. S. McEachran and F. R. Foote. This crew runs us to Helena, 297 miles. Ten miles from Hope we cross Clark's Fork, a branch of the Columbia River,

W. B. HALE, CONDUCTOR NORTHERN PACIFIC RAILWAY.

and through the gathering darkness we can see that we have entered a wild and rocky region, the road winding around and among mountain ranges and snow-capped peaks, following the course of the stream we just crossed for 60 miles.

Captain Gilbert and his brakemen are lively, interesting company, and entertain us during the evening with anecdotes and stories of Western life. "Are you troubled much with tramps, captain?" some one asks, as Conductor Gilbert, during the conversation, made some allusion to the profession. "They do not give us much real trouble," is the reply, "yet they are a matter of concern, for we are never without them, and need to be constantly on guard; there is always a Wandering Willie around somewhere, and you never know what mischief he may be up to. There are at least a dozen on this train to-night. The trucks are full and several on top of the cars." This is rather startling information, and I notice Brother Sheppard clap his hand on his right hip pocket to make sure the "critter" is there, and Alfalfa quietly unlocks the cupboard door, where "our artillery" is kept. I see no sign of fear on the serene countenance of Captain Gilbert and believe we're not in danger; yet Brothers Maxwell and Terry start through the train to make sure the vestibule doors are barred and step traps fastened down. At Trout Creek, a small station 48 miles from Hope, we stopped for water, and F. Hartman, roadmaster of the Missoula and Hope Division, got aboard and went with us to Horse Plains. It is now near midnight, and making my way from the smoker to the "Marco" I turn in, wondering how the poor fellows who are hanging on to the brake beams are enjoying themselves, for Bailey with the "438" is switching them around the curves at a pretty lively rate.

## FRIDAY, MAY 28th.

Our arrival in Helena at six o'clock this morning and the announcement of an early breakfast soon has everybody astir. After breakfast we bid adieu to jolly, wholesouled Captain Gilbert and his genial crew, and under the escort of Assistant General Passenger Agent W. Stuart, Assistant General Ticket Agent C. E. Dutton, and Conductor Dodds, of the Northern Pacific Railway, and Messrs. E. Flaherty and H. D. Palmer, of Helena Board of Trade, start out to see the town. Our time is limited, for we are scheduled to leave at twelve o'clock, and it is impossible to give all the interesting features of this remarkable city the attention they deserve. Helena is a wealthy town; it is located in the centre of one of the richest mining districts in the world; it is the capital of Montana and the county seat of Lewis and Clarke County, with a population of about 14,000; it is up to date in its financial, educational, and religious institutions, and both private residences and public buildings are models of architectural symmetry, strength, and beauty. A military post named Fort Harrison has recently been established here which will be one of the principal points for the quartering of troops in the Northwest. A ride of almost three miles on the electric line through this interesting city brings us to the Hotel Broadwater and "Natatorium," where the celebrated hot springs are located. We are given the freedom of the bathing pool, which is one of the largest and finest under cover in the world. The most of our party take advantage of the treat, and for an hour the waters of the pool are almost churned into foam by the sportive antics of the crowd, whose capers afford great entertainment and amusement for those who do not care to "get into the swim" with the rest. This place is much resorted to by tourists, and invalids are said to be much benefited by bathing in the waters of these hot springs, which are strongly impregnated with sulphur, salt, and iron and heated by Nature's process to a very pleasant temperature.

Leaving the Natatorium we are invited to the immense brewery establishment of Nicholas Kessler, near by, to await the coming of our train, which is to be brought here for us, as the railroad runs within a short distance of the place. Mr. Kessler is a former Pennsylvanian, one of those hospitable, generous, big-hearted Pennsylvania Dutchmen, and when he learned we hailed from his native State his pleasure was greater than he was able to express and his generosity almost boundless. In the fine pavilion adjoining his establishment he spread us a sumptuous lunch and seemed aggrieved that we didn't eat and drink all that was placed before us, which was enough for 500 people. When at last our train comes and we bid the old gentleman farewell there are tears in his eyes as he tells us how happy he is that we called to see him, and that he would never forget the Pennsylvania Railroad conductors. He accompanies us over to the train (so do several of his men with boxes on their shoulders), and as we steam away and leave behind us the city of Helena and our generous-hearted new-made friends, we notice in the "refreshment corner" of our combined car a pile of boxes bearing the trade mark of

"Nic" Kessler, and another box containing fine oranges that bears the mark of H. S. Hepner, a merchant of Helena.

The space between the ice chests beneath the dining car is vacant; our mascot has fled, having ridden in that uncomfortable position for 782 miles.

It is 12.55 P. M. Helena time when we leave here for Butte over the Montana Central branch of the Great Northern Railway. We have G. N. engine No. 458, Engineer Pete Leary, Fireman R. Hanna, Conductor M. Sweeney, Brakemen F. W. Minshall and F. J. Chapman, who take us to Butte, a distance of 75 miles. As a guest we have with us Trainmaster J. W. Donovan, of the Montana Central, who will accompany us to Butte. We find Mr. Donovan an agreeable and entertaining gentleman who tells us much that is interesting of the country through which we are passing. "This branch was built," says Mr. Donovan, "for almost the sole purpose of developing the mining interests of the country. You will see very little of any other industry from here to Butte than mining."

After leaving Clancy we ascend a steep grade, from which we look down into a pretty valley that Mr. Donovan tells us is called Prickly Pear Cañon. Passing Amazon we follow Boulder River for 12 miles as it courses through the beautiful valley of the same name. Four miles from Amazon we pass through Boulder and can see that it is a thriving town. "Boulder is the county seat of Jefferson County," says Mr. Donovan, "and has a population of about 1200. It ranks as one of the important cities of Montana, being in the centre of a rich mining region."

This is a wonderful mining district through which we are passing, all the hills and mountain sides being literally honeycombed with the gaping mouths of mines. Eight miles from Boulder we come to the town of Basin, "the largest city," says Mr. Donovan, "in Jefferson County, having a population of about 200 more than Boulder." The railroad runs close to the ruins of what had apparently been a large building recently destroyed by fire, and we inquire of Mr. Donovan what it had been. "Two years ago," he replies, "the Basin and Bay State Smelting Company erected an immense plant that was destroyed by fire as soon as it was in operation. To build and equip the plant cost over $100,000, and its destruction was not only a heavy loss but a serious blow to the mining industries of Basin and all the adjacent country; but I hear it is to be rebuilt if the output and value of the ore in this section will warrant it."

Our progress has become very slow and engine No. 458 is laboring very hard. "We are now ascending a grade," says Mr. Donovan, "of 116 feet to the mile and have eight miles to go before we reach the summit." It is a tedious climb, but we do not weary of viewing the wondrous mountain scenery. As we slowly approach the top of the grade we obtain an excellent view of Bison River Cañon, an exceedingly wild, rugged, and picturesque region. At last we reach the summit at an altitude of 6350 feet above sea level; this is the dividing line between the Atlantic and Pacific slopes. From this point the waters flow westward to the Pacific and eastward to the Atlantic Oceans. I look at my watch; it is 7.55 P. M. in Philadelphia and 5.55 here. We now make better time, and in twenty minutes we arrive in Butte, and are met by Brother O. L. Chapman, C. C., and Brother H. C. Grey, secretary and treasurer of Butte Division No. 294, also Brothers J. H. Dunn and A. H. Elliott, of same division, who introduce us to Major Dawson, "the man who knows everybody in Butte," and to Mr. J. R. Wharton, manager of Butte Street Railway, who gives us the freedom of his lines. Our people are escorted by the kind brothers who met us, by carriages and street cars, to the Butte Hotel, where refreshments are served, after which we are loaded into two large band wagons and driven through the principal streets of the city. Butte is a wonderful city, worth a trip across the continent to see. It is strictly a mining town and has a population of over 38,000. It is situated near the headwaters of Clark's Fork of the Columbia River, on the west slope of the dividing range of the Rocky Mountains. Butte is the county seat of Silver Bow County, a county marvelously rich in its mineral products, the aggregate value of its gold, silver, and copper product for one year reaching the enormous sum of $9,060,917.59; and yet it is claimed the mining industry in this district is still in its infancy.

Butte is a city of fine, substantial buildings that are up to date in style and beauty of architecture, and yet it is a bald and barren town, for not a tree, a leaf, a bush, a flower, or a blade of grass can we see anywhere within the length or breadth of its limits. It is surrounded on every hand by smoking smelters and grinning mines, and its streets are filled with rugged, stalwart miners. The eight-hour system of labor is in vogue here, and the mines and smelters run day and night. The great

Anaconda Mine, owned and operated by the Anaconda Company, the richest mining corporation in the world, extends, we are told, under the very centre of the city of Butte, the Butte Hotel standing directly over it. The pay rolls of the mining industries of Butte aggregate $1,500,000 yearly. We are driven out to the Colorado Smelter, and on the way pass the Centennial Brewery, where a short stop is made to obtain some souvenirs. We are shown through the great smelter, and when we come out it has grown quite dark. Our drivers are old stagers and understand handling the reins. To one wagon are attached six white horses, driven by W. M. McIntyre, of the New York Life Insurance Company, and to the other wagon are four bays, driven by Hanks Monk, a well-known character of the West. Hanks is an old stage driver, and claims to be a son of the celebrated Hanks Monk of Horace Greeley and Mark Twain fame. Mr. Monk tells us that he is a Mormon, and a deacon in Salt Lake City Church, but has only one wife, and has found one to be plenty. He is a genial, good-hearted fellow, who, notwithstanding the hardships of his rugged life of fifty-seven years, looks but forty. Hank claims he followed the trail for many years and never got far astray, but he will have to acknowledge that he got off the trail once, when he ran the wagon load of Pennsylvania Railroad conductors into a sand bank in going from the Colorado Smelter to the station in Butte on the night of May 28th, 1897. Hanks, however, redeemed himself by the dexterous and graceful manner in which he guided those bewildered horses until he struck the proper trail again, and brought us to the station all O. K. It is 10 o'clock P. M. in Butte and time for our train to start. We bid our kind and generous friends and brothers adieu and get aboard. Engine No. 305, in charge of Engineer J. Else, is drawing us, and Conductor J. A. West has charge of the train; C. Dunham is our brakeman. We have as a guest on the train Mr. H. E. Dunn, traveling agent of the Oregon Short Line. After a delay of an hour at Silver Bow, waiting to get a helper engine to assist up a grade, we start on our way again at 1.15 A. M. Eastern (11.15 P. M. Mountain) time, and I make my way to my berth in the "Marco."

### SATURDAY, MAY 29th.

Was awakened this morning between two and three o'clock by a jar that almost tumbled me out of bed; thought at first our train had left the track and had run into the side of a mountain; I lay quiet a moment, expecting another crash. It didn't come, and I realized our train was standing still. "Guess I was dreaming," I said to myself, as I reach over, raise the window blind, and look out. A freight train is moving past and our train is motionless. Mrs. S. is awake, and my movement informs her that I am in the same condition. "What was that?" she quietly asks, referring to the shock that awakened us. "I don't know, my dear, but I'm sure it was something," I reply, satisfied now that it wasn't a dream. We believe the danger is over; that there is nothing to worry about, and are soon asleep again.

Arose this morning about the usual time and find we have just left Pocatello, Idaho, 262 miles from Butte City. We have come through much interesting country while asleep, and have missed seeing the beautiful Idaho Falls. The shaking up we received last night was caused by Engineer Oram coupling engine No. 760 to our train at Lima. Oram miscalculated the distance and banged into our train with more force than he intended. At Pocatello engine No. 760 is exchanged for O. S. L. engine No. 735, with Engineer J. Andrews and Fireman Standrod in the cab, Conductor G. W. Surman and Brakeman H. Hewett, who run us to Ogden, 134 miles.

Pocatello is located in Fort Hall, Indian Reservation, and while passing through this district we see a number of the natives. Much of the country is level and covered with sage brush and bunch grass, constituting immense cattle ranges, with here and there a plot of land under cultivation, watered by irrigation, while at a distance on either side can be seen great ranges of snow-capped mountains. We are reminded of Chester County and home as we see the familiar name of "Oxford" above a little station door as we fly past, midway between Dayton and Cannon. We cross the State Line and enter Utah. Coming to Cache Junction, we are in view of Bear River, that feeds the great irrigating canal constructed by the Bay State Canal and Irrigating Company at a cost of $2,000,000. This canal is about 80 miles long, the waters from which irrigate many thousand acres of land; it is converting this dry and barren desert country into a land of fertility, fruits, and flowers.

As we approach Ogden this great improvement is very noticeable in the beautiful, productive farms and homesteads that are seen on every hand. The most of the settlers through this locality, we are told, are Mormons, but the aspect of their condition and surroundings show them to be a thrifty, industrious, enterprising people. We arrive in Ogden at 11.20 A. M., where a stop of only twenty minutes is allowed. We are met by Conductor E. S. Croker, C. C. of Wasatch Division No. 124, and J. H. McCoy, of same division, who is yardmaster for the Union Pacific Railroad at this point. Much as we desire to make a tour of this interesting city, our limited time will not allow it, but we can see that it is a thriving business place. It is situated on the western slope of the Wasatch Range, at an elevation of 4301 feet above sea level, on a triangle formed by the Weber and Ogden Rivers, which, uniting a short distance west of the city, flow across the famous historic valley and empty into the Great Salt Lake.

At Ogden, going west, the Union Pacific Railroad time changes from Mountain to Pacific time. At 1.40 P. M. Eastern (11.40 A. M. Mountain) time we start on our way again with R. G. W. engine No. 41, in charge of Engineer J. Stewart, Conductor George King, and Brakeman J. Crompton. From Ogden to Salt Lake City we are in continual view of the Great Salt Lake, and pass a number of evaporating dams, where a large amount of salt is procured through the process of evaporation. We arrive in Salt Lake City at 12.30 P. M. Mountain time, and leaving the train we are again hustled into wagons and driven over the city, the places of interest being pointed out and explained by the drivers. Time and space will not permit me to note and describe all the interesting features of this historic and truly wonderful city. We passed through the famous Eagle Gateway and halted on a lofty promontory over-

"DAN," SALT LAKE CITY RAILROAD STATION, UTAH.

GRAVE OF BRIGHAM YOUNG, SALT LAKE CITY, UTAH.

looking Temple Square, where we had a grand view of the magnificent $10,000,000 Mormon Temple. Near the Temple is the Tabernacle, an immense, singular-looking affair, with a roof like the shell of a huge tortoise. We are shown the Lion House and Beehive House, former residences of Brigham Young and his large family, and pass the grave where the remains of the great leader lie. It is a plain, ordinary-looking mound, inclosed with a common iron fence. The great monument erected to the imperishable fame of Brigham Young is this beautiful, remarkable city that he founded fifty years ago. For thirty years he was the temporal and religious leader of his people here, and Salt Lake City was almost strictly Mormon. It is exclusive no longer, for of its present population of 65,000 about one-half, we are told, are Gentiles or Christians. "The Christian Science faith is making rapid advances," says our driver, "and many Mormons are being converted to that creed." Brigham Young was the father of fifty-six children; when he died he left seventeen widows, sixteen sons, and twenty-eight daughters to mourn his loss, many of whom are living yet.

We are driven through Liberty Park, where is still standing the first flour mill built in Utah. Returning to the train we get dinner, after which our people scatter through the city to see the sights and gather more souvenirs. We are all impressed with the beauty and regularity of the streets, which all cross at right angles, are 132 feet wide, including the sidewalks, which are 20 feet in width, bordered with beautiful Lombardy poplar and locust trees. Along each side of the street flows a clear, cold stream of water, which, with the beauty of the trees and the sweet fragrance of the locust blossoms, gives to the city an all-pervading air of coolness, comfort, and repose which is exceedingly inviting to a warm and weary tourist. The hour grows late and the time arrives to return to our train, which is sidetracked for occupancy at the Rio Grande Western depot. Several of our party gather at the corner of Main and Second South Street to await the coming of a trolley car that will convey us to the depot, about two miles away. According to the schedule of the line a car should pass every ten minutes, but to-night must be an exception, for it is forty-five minutes before our car arrives, and several of the party have started to walk. It is near midnight when we reach our train and turn in for the night.

### SUNDAY, MAY 30th.

We are all astir bright and early this morning, and after breakfast, through the courtesy of the managers of the Saltair and Los Angeles Railway, we are tendered a trip on their line to Saltair, one of the latest attractions on the Great Salt Lake, 10 miles from the city. We leave the Rio Grande Western depot at 9.30 on a Saltair and Los Angeles train with engine No. 2, Engineer A. M. Clayton, Fireman John Little, Conductor Joseph Risley, Brakeman F. T. Bailey. We have a thirty minutes' pleasant ride through an interesting country. The first few miles we pass through a district of cozy homes, surrounded by fertile fields and gardens, the result of industry and irrigation; then come great level stretches of country, utilized as grazing ground, upon which can be seen feeding thousands of sheep. As we approach the "Great Dead Sea" of America we see that gathering salt is the chief industry, and we pass many basins or dams where hundreds of tons of this useful commodity are procured through the process of evaporation. Arriving at our destination we find Saltair is a magnificent mammoth pavilion built on the waters of Great Salt Lake, 4000 feet from shore. A track resting upon piles connects the pavilion with the mainland, and over this our train is run.

Saltair was erected in 1893 by Salt Lake capitalists at an expense of $250,000. It is of Moorish style of architecture, 1115 feet long, 335 feet wide, and 130 feet high from the water to the top of the main tower. It is over a quarter of a mile from shore and rests upon 2500 ten-inch piling or posts driven firmly into the bottom of the lake. It contains 620 bath houses or dressing rooms, and connected with each room is an apartment equipped with a fresh-water shower bath. Visitors who wish to drink or lunch or lounge will find at their disposal a fine apartment 151 by 153 feet, furnished with convenient tables and comfortable chairs, or if it is their desire to "trip the light fantastic toe," they will find the ball room always open, a fine piano, and dancing floor 140 by 250 feet. At night this wonderful place is lighted by electricity, there being 1250 incandescent and 40 arc lamps, and above all, in the centre of the building, there is an arc light of 2000 candle power. The bathing season has not opened yet and the water is said to be cold, but many of us have a strong desire to take a plunge in this remarkable and famous lake. The temperature of the water is found to be about 75 degrees, and opinion is divided as to whether or not it is too cold. Manager Wyman takes off his shoes and stockings and dabbles in the water. "It is not cold," he exclaims, "and I'm going in;" and procuring a bathing suit he is soon splashing in the brine. His example is rapidly followed by others, until the majority of our party, both men and women, are floating and floundering around in water so salt that its density enables one to swim and float with ease, but you are helpless when you attempt to place your feet upon the bottom; the water within the bathing limits averages about five feet in depth, and the bottom is hard, smooth, and sandy. "If you get water in your mouth spit it out, and if you get it in your eyes don't rub them," is the advice given us by the bath attendant. If you get this water in your mouth you want to spit it out right away; that part of the caution is unnecessary, for it is the worst stuff I ever tasted. If you get it in your eyes you will want to rub them, and rub them hard, but don't do it, and you will be surprised how soon the intense smarting will cease.

We love to swim and dive and splash and sport in the water, and have bathed in many places, but in a brine like this never before. In fact, it has been said that nothing like it can be found anywhere this side of the Dead Sea of Palestine. We remained in the water for an hour and all thoroughly enjoyed its peculiar qualities. Several of the party who never swam before did so to-day, but it was because they couldn't help it, and it was better than a circus to see them. Not one of us regret or will ever forget out trip to Saltair and our bath in Great Salt Lake. Strange as it may seem, this great inland sea occupies an altitude 4000 feet higher than the Atlantic and Pacific Oceans. It is 93 miles long, with an average width of 43 miles, containing almost 4000 square miles. It is shallow compared with the depth of other large bodies of water, its deepest places measuring but 60 feet. A number of islands rise out of its waters, the largest being Stansbury and Antelope, near its southern shore. It is between these two islands that beautiful, destined-to-be-celebrated Saltair is located.

Returning, we arrive at the Rio Grande Western depot about 12.30, and after partaking of lunch in our dining car we go in a body to attend services in the Mormon Tabernacle. They were looking for us, for we had been invited to come, and we find a section of vacant seats awaiting us near the centre of the immense auditorium. We are all favorably impressed with what we see and hear, the Mormon manner of worship being not unlike that of any other church. So far as we can discern, the speakers make no effort to expound any particular or peculiar creed or doctrine, but preach charity, love, and duty to one another and obedience to the laws of God, which is a religion good enough for the entire world. An attractive feature of the service is the singing, the choir consisting of 400 voices, accompanied by the music of what is claimed to be one of the largest church organs in the world, and led by a gentleman highly skilled in his profession, who manages his great concourse of singers with remarkable accuracy and precision. This music is aided and enhanced by the peculiar and marvelous acoustic properties of the building, which seems to convey and distribute sound in such a wonderful manner that the entire edifice is filled with the grand and charming melody. We are all delighted and highly appreciate the privilege of having been allowed to visit this, one of the noted wonders of this famous Mormon city. The Tabernacle is an oddly-constructed building, 250 feet long, 150 feet wide, and 80 feet high, covered with an oval-shaped roof that, without any visible support except where it rests upon the walls, spans the vast auditorium beneath, which will seat over 8000 people.

The place was well filled to-day, and we are told that it is not unusual to have a congregation of 10,000 within the inclosure during Sabbath service. There are twenty double doors nine feet in width, which open outward, like the great doors of a barn, and the floor being on a level with the ground outside, the vast congregation is enabled to make its exit in a very few minutes without crowding or confusion.

The services being over, we soon find ourselves outside the building, but still within the inclosure that constitutes Temple Square. This square or "block," containing about ten acres, is surrounded by a wall two feet thick and fourteen feet high, composed of adobe bricks built upon a foundation of stone. Four great gates, one on each side, lead into the inclosure, which is ornamented with fine shade trees and beautiful flowers, and contains the three famous buildings of the Mormons, or "Latter Day Saints," as they prefer to be called. The Tabernacle, where regular service is held each Sabbath, is the only edifice to which the public is admitted. Assembly Hall, a large granite building of unique design, erected in 1880 at a cost of $90,000, is used exclusively by Church officials for special meet-

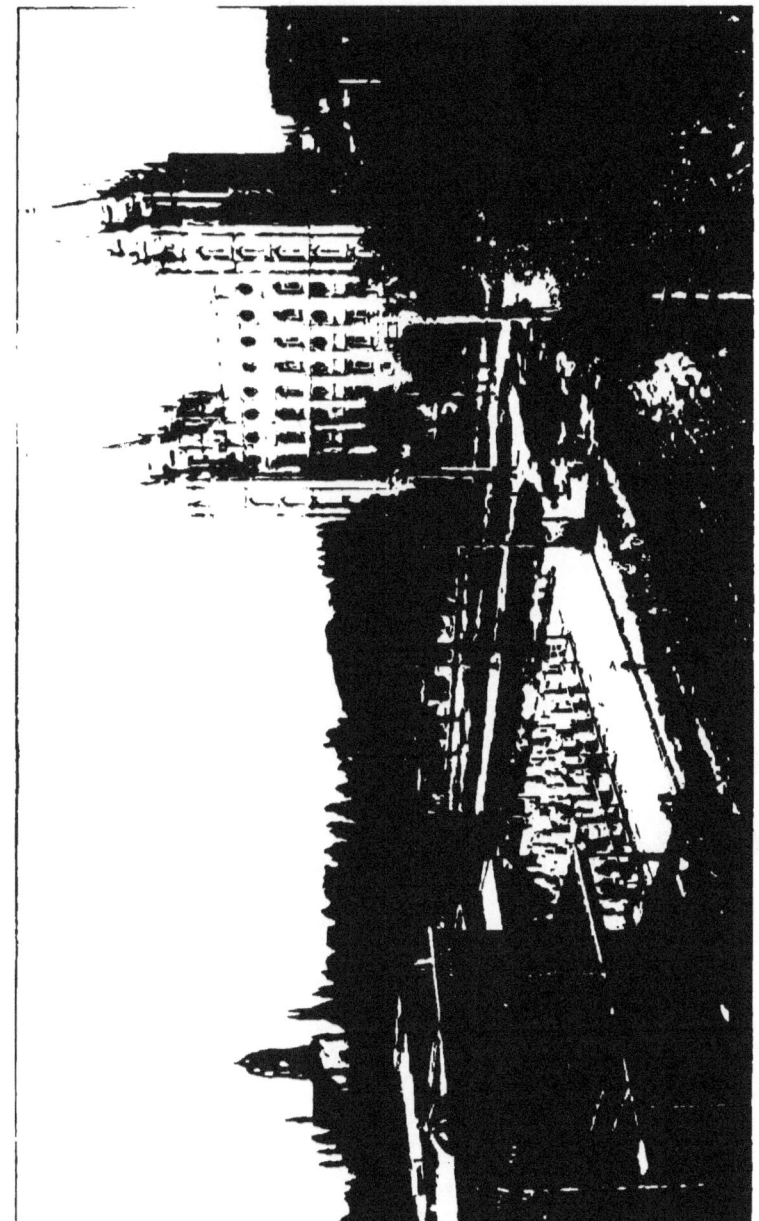

THE MORMON TEMPLE AND SQUARE, SALT LAKE CITY.

ings pertaining to the business of the Church. The Temple, a grand granite structure, the building and furnishing of which, we are told, has cost many millions of dollars, is as a sealed book to the outside world. Its interior is regarded as holy, consecrated ground, that has never been contaminated by an "unbeliever's" presence. To admit a Gentile within its walls would be a fearful desecration. We cannot get inside, and gaze in admiration and curiosity upon its grand and massive walls, wondering what mighty mysteries are hidden within. Near the Temple that he designed and the corner stone of which he laid stands the statue of Brigham Young.

Leaving the grounds, our party scatters, some returning to the train and others strolling around the city. The sun shines very hot, but it is cool and refreshing in the shade. Mrs. S. and myself make a call on Mrs. Catharine Palmer, residing on State Street, a sister of Mr. C. K. Dolby, of Delaware County, Pennsylvania, an acquaintance of mine, who requested me to call on his sister had I the opportunity while in Salt Lake City. We are cordially received and spend a pleasant hour with Mr. and Mrs. Palmer, who are well advanced in years and very comfortably fixed. Their residence is surrounded by great maple trees, planted by Mr. Palmer many years ago, and he now loves to sit on his porch under their grateful shade and enjoy the fruits of his well-spent days of industry and toil.

On our return to the depot I encounter a party of the "boys" under the escort of Mr. James Devine, chief of Salt Lake City fire department, an acquaintance of Brother Leary's, who are starting on a little tour through the town.  I join them, and boarding an electric car we make a pleasant trip and are shown many places of interest.  Mr. Devine is an excellent guide and entertains us with a number of anecdotes and stories of the people and their customs.  "Who is the present head of the Mormon Church, Mr. Devine?" I ask.  "An old gentleman by the name of W. Woodruff," replies Mr. Devine, "but it will not be long, I think, before they will need another, for Mr. Woodruff is past ninety years of age.  A short time ago, in commemoration of his ninetieth birthday, a family reunion was held, at which gathering his children, grandchildren, and greatgrandchildren numbered 90, one direct descendant for each year of his life.  The old man is quite wealthy and owns some of the most fertile land in the State of Utah, if not in the world.  I know it to be a fact that an experiment was made last year with an acre of his land to determine the amount of potatoes that can be raised per acre under favorable conditions, and that acre produced the extraordinary yield of 800 bushels.  A like experiment in producing wheat resulted in the unprecedented yield of 82 bushels." We can hardly credit this, but Mr. Devine declares it is true.  One of the "boys" has been holding a letter in his hand, addressed to some friend in the East, and for some time has been waiting for a chance to deposit it in a letter box without getting left; at last he sees a chance, and quickly springing from the car when it stops at a corner to discharge some passengers, he tries to find an opening in what he supposes is a United States receptacle for letters.  "Hold on, there," exclaims Chief Devine, "I have a key for that if you want to get into it." It is a fire-alarm box into which our brother is trying to insert his epistle. "Twenty-five dollars fine for tampering with a fire alarm in this town," says Brother Maxwell, as the abashed victim of the mistake returns to the car. "Yer-hef-ner bizness to monkey with it," chided Brother Schuler; but the proper place is soon found and the letter safely mailed.

We called on Jacob Moritz, president of the Utah Brewing Company, of Salt Lake City, who showed us over his immense establishment and entertained us in a very generous manner. During the conversation, Mr. Moritz, while speaking about the decline of polygamy on account of the vigorous enforcement of the law that forbids a plurality of wives, recited an incident that came under his observation a short time since. An old Mormon having several wives fell a victim to the stern mandate of the law. Being under indictment for a criminal offense results in disfranchisement, but the old gentleman did not know he could not vote. Pending his trial an election occurred and the old man went to the polls to cast his ballot, but was sternly challenged. He was dumfounded at first, but was soon made to understand why he was denied the privileges of citizenship. Raising his right hand toward Heaven he exclaimed, "Gentlemen, you won't allow me to vote, but, thank God, I have twenty-four sons who can vote." "That's a family of boys to be proud of," remarked Brother Leary. "If they were illegally procured," added Brother Reilly. Mr. Moritz offered a fine cut-glass goblet to the one who could come nearest guessing the number of drams it would hold. Brother Waddington got closest to it and carried off the prize.

Bidding adieu to our kind host, we returned to our

train and found dinner ready in the dining car. Chief Devine returned and took dinner with us. We also had with us as a guest Mr. Nymphas C. Murdock, of Charlestown, Wasatch County, Utah. Brother Barrett met Mr. Murdock at the Tabernacle services this afternoon, and becoming interested in his conversation invited him to visit our train. Mr. Murdock is a bishop in the Mormon Church and an intelligent and highly entertaining gentleman. Fifty years ago, when but ten years of age, he came with his parents, who were followers of Brigham Young, on that famous journey to the Great Salt Lake Valley. He has been identified with the Church since its establishment here, and was the first settler in Charlestown, which is located about 35 miles west of Salt Lake City, and he has been postmaster there for 31 years. Mr. Murdock made no effort to intrude upon us any of the peculiar doctrines or beliefs of his Church, but answered all our questions in a frank and pleasant manner, giving us a great deal of useful and interesting information. "Tell us something about your Temple, Mr. Murdock," I requested, "and why you consider it too holy for visitors to enter?" "The Temple is considered holy because it has been consecrated to holy creeds and devoted to sacred objects," answered Mr. Murdock in a solemn, quiet tone. "The spirits of the dead assemble in the Temple to commune with living friends." "If that is so I don't blame them for excluding the public," I said to myself, "for if there is anything that will make a spirit scoot it is the presence of an unbeliever," but I remained perfectly quiet, for I felt there was more coming. "We have a creed," continued Mr. Murdock, "that declares the living can be wedded to the dead, and it is in the Temple that this most sacred of all ceremonies is solemnized and performed." "I can't see how it is possible," I quietly remarked. "I will explain," Mr. Murdock gently said; "to the 'believer' it is very plain and simple. Suppose, for instance, I am betrothed to a woman who sickens and dies before we are married; if she truly loved me in life her spirit will meet me at the Temple altar, where marriage rites will be performed that will unite us for all eternity." I really think Mr. Murdock is a good and honest man and believes what he told us, but to us the whole matter seemed like an interesting fairy story—very pretty, but outside the realm of truth and reason. There were some pertinent questions in my mind I felt like asking, but did not wish to injure the feelings or offend a kind and entertaining guest, and so we bid him good-bye and let him depart in peace.

A number of our people went over to Fort Douglas this afternoon and were highly pleased with the trip. George "Alfalfa" was along and met an old chum over there in the person of William Barnes. William was a messenger in the employ of Mayor Fitler, Philadelphia, when George and he were buddies. He likes army life first rate and George says he is a good soldier. The troops at Fort Douglas are all colored, commanded by white officers. We are scheduled to leave this evening at nine o'clock, and it is drawing near the time; our train is at the station and Manager Wyman has ascertained that our people are all "on deck." We must not forget "Dan," the pet bear at the Rio Grande Western depot. He was captured several years ago when a cub and has been confined in a pen near the station ever since. He

is a fine big fellow now, and has been faring well since
our visit, for no one of our party thinks of passing the
pen of Dan without giving him some sweetmeats, of
which he is very fond. My last thoughts are of Dan,
for finding I have some lumps of sugar and a few cakes
in my pocket, I hasten to his pen and give them to him,
and return just in time to get aboard. We leave
promptly at 11.00 P. M. Eastern (9.00 P. M. Mountain)
time, over the Rio Grande Western Railway, bound for
Grand Junction, with the same engine and crew that
brought us from Ogden to Salt Lake City. As a guest
we have with us Train Supervisor Frank Selgrath, who
will go with us to Grand Junction. At Clear Creek, 83
miles from Salt Lake City, we get a ten-wheel engine,
No. 132, to help us up a six-mile grade with a rise of
200 feet to the mile. This is a fine, picturesque country,
we are told, through which we are passing, but not being able to see in the dark, we cannot judge of its beauty,
and finding it is near midnight I hie away to my little
bed and am soon fast asleep.

### MONDAY, MAY 31st.

Awakened this morning about six o'clock by Mrs. S.
remarking, "I never saw the beat! Who would believe
that so much of our country is desert?" I thought she
was talking in her sleep, but turning over I find her gaz-
ing out of the window at the rapidly-fleeting landscape.
We have drifted away from the mountains and rocks and
are crossing a level, barren plain. For miles we see no
sign of habitation or cultivation, but now in the distance
we catch sight of an irrigating canal, with here and there
a plot of land under cultivation whose fertility and verd-

CHAS. I. HOOPER OF THE DENVER AND RIO GRANDE RAILROAD.

ure break the hard lines of the desert monotony. We pass a station and upon the name board we see the word "Fruita," a singular name, we think, for a station; but in the two seconds' glance we have of its surroundings we can but feel that it is appropriate. Irrigating ditches, fertile fields, thrifty orchards, and blooming gardens are all seen in that fleeting glance, and we are more than ever impressed with the fact that it needs but water to convert these desert tracts into verdant fields. A number of our people are astir, and we too "turn out." We find we are in Colorado, having crossed the State line at Utaline, a little station 35 miles west of Grand Junction, which we are now approaching, and where we arrive about seven o'clock. We halt here only long enough to change engines, but in our brief stay we can see that Grand Junction is quite a town. It has a population of about 4000; is located at the confluence of the Gunnison and Grand Rivers, with an elevation of 4500 feet; it is quite a railway centre, being the terminus of both the broad and narrow-gauge lines of the Denver and Rio Grande, the Rio Grande Western and the Colorado Midland Railways.

At 9.08 A. M. Eastern (7.08 A. M. Mountain) time we leave Grand Junction, on the Denver and Rio Grande Railroad, with engine No. 522, Engineer "Cyclone" Thompson, Fireman Bert Roberts, Conductor William M. Newman, Brakemen J. Grout and O. McCullough. Conductor Hugh Long, of Salida Division No. 132, and Charles E. Hooper, advertising agent of the Denver and Rio Grande Railroad, met our train at Grand Junction, and we find them a pleasing and entertaining addition to our party. They present us with descriptive time tables, illustrated pamphlets, and souvenir itineraries of our trip over the wonderful scenic route of the Denver and Rio Grande Railroad. From Grand Junction to Glenwood Springs we follow the Grand River through the Valley of the Grand, amid grand and beautiful scenery. As we approach Glenwood Springs and pass the little stations of Rifle and Antlers, Brother Sloane grows very enthusiastic, for this is a noted hunting district, with which our brother is familiar. From Newcastle to Glenwood Springs, a distance of 12 miles, we traverse closely the north banks of the Grand River, and parallel with the tracks of the Colorado Midland Railroad on the opposite side.

Arriving at Glenwood Springs at 9.40 A. M., we go direct from the train to the springs under the escort of Mr. Hooper, who has made arrangements to give our party free access to the bathing establishment, where we are very courteously received, and each one who desires to bathe is furnished with a suit and a dressing room. Steps lead down into the pool, which is about an acre in size and filled with warm, sulphurous water to the depth of four to five feet. The hot water, at a temperature of 120 degrees, gushes into the pool on one side at the rate of about 2000 gallons per minute, and on the opposite side an ice-cold mountain stream pours in at about the same rate, keeping the water at a pleasant bathing temperature.

We spent an hour in the pool and enjoyed it mightily. How much fun we had we can never tell, but we know we had fun, and other people knew it, too, for the following item appeared in to-day's *Avalanche*, an afternoon Glenwood Springs paper:—

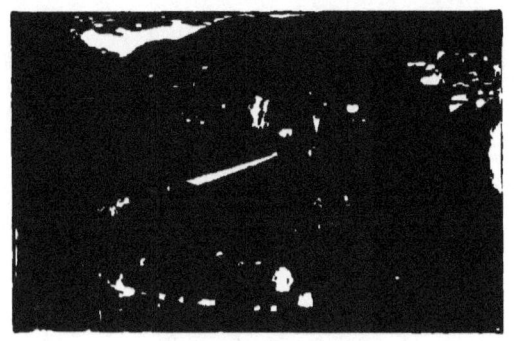

BATHING POOL AT GLENWOOD SPRINGS, COLORADO.

IN THE POOL AT GLENWOOD SPRINGS.

"CONDUCTORS IN THE POOL.

"The Pennsylvania Railroad conductors who arrived in Glenwood Springs this morning from the West had more fun in the pool than a lot of wild Indians. Their shouts of mirth and their laughter could be hear at Cardiff, three miles south. If the Indians ever had as much fun in that pool as those Pennsylvania Railroad conductors, then, Wampam woopham longheir spookham."

We all feel that this item does us great honor, but we are puzzled for awhile to understand the meaning of the closing expression, until one of our party who had made a study of savage classic lore interpreted it as meaning, "Yankem, spankem, daredevil blankem."

After leaving the pool, another hour was spent in visiting the sulphur springs and vapor cave and in writing and mailing letters. The latter we did in the beautiful Hotel Colorado, which is located near the bathing establishment and is said to be one of the finest-equipped hotels between the Atlantic and Pacific. The Grand River separates the baths from the town, and is crossed by a double-decker bridge, the lower deck for vehicles, the upper for pedestrians. We recrossed the bridge and after a short wait for our train to be brought to us we again got aboard, and at 3.00 P. M. Eastern (1.00 P. M. Mountain) time left Glenwood Springs bound for Salida.

For 16 miles we wind through the cañon of the Grand River, and view with feelings of admiration and awe those towering walls of rock of such peculiar construction and varied colors that we wonder what remarkable process of Nature could have ever formed them thus.

At Gypsum, 25 miles from Glenwood Springs, Grand River disappears from view and we come in sight of Eagle River, following it for several miles. We pass great beds of lava and can see, away in the distance, a burned and blackened course where the lava had flowed down a chasm in the mountain, perhaps thousands of years ago. On the plateaus, at the foot of towering cliffs, are numerous little farms in a thrifty state of cultivation. We stop at Minturn to change engines, and bid "Cyclone" Thompson and his trusty fireman, Bert Roberts, good-bye.

We leave in a few minutes with engine No. 524. Engineer Al. Philliber and Fireman Charley Wilcox are in the cab, "Billy" Newman and his brakemen remain with us. Conductor Newman is a member of Denver Division No. 44 and an enthusiastic lover of the order. He is a model conductor and an entertaining companion. E. A. Thayer, Esq., superintendent of hotel, dining, and restaurant service, is our guest from Glenwood Springs to Salida, and we find him an interesting gentleman. Brother Dougherty has found an old friend in Brother Hugh Long, and he has much enjoyment in his company. Charley Hooper is everybody's friend and always has an admiring, interested group around him, and if we could only remember all that Charley tells us we could write an intensely interesting volume. He is perfectly familiar with all of this wonderful country and is an exceedingly interesting companion.

Soon after leaving Minturn we enter Eagle River Cañon, whose sloping, pine-fringed walls rise to the height of over 2000 feet on either side, almost shutting out the light of day. A heavy shower adds to the gloom, but does not detract from the interest, for these mighty mountain sides are honeycombed with hundreds of mines and dotted with the cabins of the miners. It is very curious and wonderful to see a human habitation hanging, as it were, a thousand feet in the air, on the side of a mountain, where it would seem a mountain goat could hardly obtain a foothold; yet there they are, and many of them—in one place an entire village of red and white cottages, so very high up that they look like miniature houses or dove cots suspended in the air. The products of the mines are lowered to the railroad tracks by means of tramways operated by endless chains or cables, and material is conveyed to the lofty residents by the same novel arrangement.

For four miles we wind up through this marvelous mountain ravine, deeply interested in the wonderful sights and scenery of this extraordinary mining industry. A short stop is made at Belden, where extensive gold mines are in operation, but so high up on the mountain side are the shafts or entrances to the mines that it is impossible to visit them in the limited time we have. Since leaving Minturn our course has been gradually upward, and we have Engineer Amberson, with helper engine No. 513, to assist us up the grade. Emerging from the famous and never-to-be-forgotten Eagle River Cañon, we shortly come to the mining town of Red Cliff. It is a lively, thrifty place of about 1000 inhabitants, has an elevation of 8671 feet, and is surrounded by grand mountain scenery. From this point Mr. Hooper directs our attention to a view of the Mount of the Holy Cross, but only a glimpse is obtained of the great white cross and then it is lost to view. "Distance lends enchantment to the view," quotes Mr. Thayer. "Do you know," he continues, "were it possible to transport you to the summit of yonder mount, 20 miles away, and set you down, you would see no semblance of a cross? You would only see rugged rocks, desolate peaks, and snow-filled ravines; you would look in vain for the sublime and typical beauty that you so easily discern 20 miles or more away. You would see, were you in a proper location, the conditions and materials that make your beautiful picture. A great valley or ravine extends down the mountain side, into which the snows of many Winters have drifted. This is one of Nature's perpetual ice houses, whose supply never becomes exhausted. Across the face of the mountain, near the summit, crossing this ravine at right angles, is another great depression or fissure, likewise filled with perpetual ice and snow. All the surroundings are rugged, rough, and broken, and you would never think of looking for the likeness of a cross in the wild, bleak desolation of ice-bound, snow-filled mountain chasms. Distance, however, obliterates the rocks and roughness and smooths the rugged features of the mountain side, and the great white cross of snow stands out in bold relief, as though formed of carved and polished marble. It is a pretty picture, and one that the imagination and sentiment of man have almost rendered sacred."

We are now approaching Tennessee Pass, and our engines are working hard as they climb the steep ascent. Our progress is slow, but so much the better, as it gives us an opportunity to contemplate and enjoy the indescribable beauty of this famous mountain scenery. We reach the pass shortly after four o'clock, at an altitude of 10,418 feet, the highest point on the main line of the Denver and Rio Grande Railroad. Here we again cross the Great Continental Divide and enter the Atlantic slope. Mr. Hooper calls our attention to a tiny stream of water flowing near the track, remarking as he does so, "That is the headwaters of the Arkansas River. We follow it for a number of miles and it will be interesting to notice it gradually increasing in size and volume as we proceed." Our course is slightly downward and our rate of speed increases. We soon reach Leadville, where we halt for half an hour. The time is insufficient to allow us to visit the town, but we get out and look around. A train of freight cars is standing on a sidetrack a short distance away, loaded with ore, and the "boys" are told to help themselves. A number avail themselves of the opportunity of procuring Leadville "specimens" for souvenirs. The pieces carried away, I imagine, contain but very little of the precious metal, for I believe, judging from the appearance, that the "specimens" are being obtained from a train load of railroad ballast. I tell Brothers Sparks and Matthews and some of the rest my convictions, but they call me a "tenderfoot" and say I "don't know a good thing when I see it." Maybe I don't, but I have a chunk of that stuff in my pocket that I will take home and exhibit to my friends as a specimen of Leadville gold quartz, and if they know no more about the material than I do they will believe it. If it is but a stone, I will prize it as a souvenir from the most noted mining camp of the West.

Leadville first became famous in 1859 as the richest gold-mining camp in Colorado, and was known as

"California Gulch." Five million dollars in gold dust were washed from the ground of this gulch the first five years after its discovery, then for fourteen years it lay almost dormant, until in 1878 rich deposits of silver were discovered. At that time the place took a new lease of life, was renamed Leadville, and has been a booming city ever since. It now has a population of 15,000 inhabitants and is the county seat of Lake County. Leadville has an elevation of 10,200 feet, enjoying the highest altitude of any city of its size in North America, if not in the world. It lies amid some of the grandest and most magnificent scenery to be found anywhere, and is surrounded by towering, snow-capped mountain peaks, whose glistening summits almost pierce the sky. We find the atmosphere cool and bracing, but so exceedingly rare that a brisk walk or short run will make you pant for breath. I found this out when I ran to the sidetrack for a piece of "ballast."

Our half hour is up and Conductor Newman and Manager Wyman are shouting "All aboard!" We scramble on, and at 7.40 P. M. Eastern (5.40 P. M. Mountain) time our train pulls out and we leave in our rear an interesting, picturesque, and famous town. At Malta, five miles from Leadville, we lay on a sidetrack ten minutes waiting for a train we meet at this point. Leaving Malta, we pass through a fertile valley, through which flows the Arkansas River, that we notice is rapidly growing larger and more turbulent. We are still running parallel with the Colorado Midland Railroad, which for miles is within fifty feet of the Denver and Rio Grande. We notice a severe storm raging on a mountain not far away, and it seems to be snowing hard at the summit.

WALTER W. TERRY, OF THE COMMITTEE.

As we pass Buena Vista, 25 miles west of Salida, the setting sun is shining upon the snow-crowned summits of the collegiate group of mountain peaks, Harvard, Yale, and Princeton, and many are the exclamations of pleasure and delight at the beauty and grandeur of the sight. These three peaks, each over 14,000 feet in height, are a part of the Sawatch Range of the Rocky Mountains. With their cloud-veiled crests wreathed in perpetual snow, those majestic, rugged giants are ever subjects of interest and pleasure to tourists; but this evening the setting sun has transformed their crowns of glistening snow into dazzling diamonds, and the veil of fleecy clouds that hang about their summits into a gorgeous canopy of purple, silver, and gold. It is a scene of transcendent loveliness and grandeur. No wonder our people are in ecstasies of delight. Mrs. Dougherty claps her hands, and Mrs. Matthews exclaims, "Jimmie, look!" Jimmie, Waddie, Oscar, and the Colonel suspend their interesting game of euchre and turn their attention for a moment to the mountains and the clouds. Mrs. Horner has such an expression of intense rapture in her face that Sam, thinking she is about to have a fit, pours a glass of ice water down her back. Mrs. Mattson says she believes she has an artist's soul, for a sight like this makes her nerves tingle and her mouth water, and the Doctor, standing near, is explaining to an interested circle the philosophy of sunshine, clouds, and colors in their relation to towering, snow-crowned peaks. Suddenly mountain views are obstructed and the light of day is almost excluded by massive walls of rock that encompass us. We have plunged into Brown's Cañon, a mighty chasm in the mountain, between whose towering cliffs there is just room enough for the Arkansas River and the railroad. For many, many years the river held undisputed sway and rushed unaccompanied and alone through this rocky, desolate gorge, till then the railroad came. The nerve and daring of the men who brought it were equal to the task. They followed the foaming river into this wild ravine and fearlessly built their tracks upon its spray-bathed banks; and now as train and river rush headlong together through this narrow, dark defile, the snort of the locomotive and rumble of the train mingles with the roar and gurgle of the tumultuous torrent.

We emerge from the cañon as suddenly as we entered it, and the broad, fertile valley of the Arkansas greets our vision. It is a pleasant change. Still following the river, we traverse the valley until at 7.55, as daylight is fading and it is growing dusk, our train comes to a stop in Salida. We are met at the station by Superintendent R. M. Ridgway, Trainmaster G. H. Barnes, and Chief Dispatcher W. Rech, of the Denver and Rio Grande Railroad, who give us a cordial welcome and kindly inform us that arrangements have been made to give us a trip to-morrow over the narrow-gauge road to Marshall Pass and return. Escorted by Mr. Hooper and Conductor Newman, a number of us start out to see the town.

Salida is a quiet, clean, orderly, picturesque little mountain town of about 3500 inhabitants. It is situated on the Arkansas River, with an elevation of 7050 feet. We accept an invitation to visit the fine parlors of the Salida Club and are royally treated by the members present. Our bosom friend and life preserver, Tom McDonald, is along, and proves to be quite an expert with the billiard cue, giving his opponent, Dr. Mattson, a hard hustle in the game they play. A party of our ladies get on our trail and overtake us at the club. They present the bachelor brothers of the party each with a miniature souvenir spoon, but give no explanation why this is done. The inference is that it is but an act of sisterly good-fellowship that needs no interpretation. Following the presentation of the spoons the ladies entertain us for half an hour with excellent singing and music on the piano. As it draws near midnight we return to our train and turn in. Some of the "boys," it is noticed, are not with us when we reach the train, and to them I will have to ascribe another line of "unwritten history."

## TUESDAY, JUNE 1st.

Everybody is up bright and early this morning, in anticipation of the promised trip up the mountains to Marshall Pass. After breakfast we board a special train on the Denver and Rio Grande Narrow-Gauge Railroad, and at 8.12 o'clock start on a novel and interesting ride of 25 miles over a road that is a marvel of engineering ingenuity and skill. It requires two engines to make the laborious ascent, which in many places is 211 feet to the mile. Our engines are No. 175, manned by Engineer Sam Roney and Fireman W. Brewster; helper engine No. 400, Engineer W. D. Yates, Fireman M. M. Smith. Conductor M. Guerin has charge of the train, and the brakemen are Tom Kelley and F. Duncan.

Five miles from Salida we reach Poncha Junction, and here the winding and climbing commences in earnest.

The weather since we started has become unfavorable; clouds obscure the sun and hide the summits of the surrounding peaks. It has commenced to rain, but the rain lasts only for a little while. As we ascend the clouds become lighter, and finally we see the sun and the sky. Looking down, the clouds and mist hide the valleys from our sight—we are above the clouds and rain; looking up, we behold the brightest, bluest sky we have ever seen; and still our course is upward. Our engines snort and cough and puff as they slowly climb and wind the spiral pathway that leads to the wind-swept summit.

As we near the top we have a magnificent unobstructed view of grand, majestic mountain scenery. Near by looms up mighty Mt. Ouray, an extinct volcano, down whose rugged sides, ages ago, the molten lava flowed; fire-scarred and grim he stands, a silent, frowning sentinel guarding the mountain pass. His companion, Mt. Shaveno, is near, his towering summit being crowned with eternal snow. Mounts Ouray and Shaveno were named in honor of the famous Ute Indian chiefs, and are everlasting monuments to the memory of a once powerful tribe.

Far in the distance, many miles to the south, can be seen, mingling with the sky and clouds, the gleaming peaks of the Sangre de Cristo Mountains, the grandest range of the Sierras. All this range of vision, from Ouray to Sangre de Cristo, is filled with picturesque valleys, timbered hills, mountain cañons, towering peaks, and glistening snow. While we are feasting our eyes upon this grandeur, suddenly it is shut out from view, for we have entered a dismal snow shed. The train stops and our journey is ended. We get out of the train,

COLONEL AND MRS. MITCHELL AT MARSHALL PASS.

THE "COMMITTEE" AT MARSHALL PASS.

and looking around, we see a door that leads from the shed, which we pass through, and find snowdrifts six feet deep and the wind blowing a gale.

I see Brother Restein snap his kodak at Colonel and Mrs. Mitchell as they bravely face the wintry blast; the committee is lined up and he also snaps at them. Steps lead to a lofty tower and a number of us ascend. Some start and turn back; the exertion makes your heart beat like a trip hammer, cuts your wind, and makes you dizzy. We who reach the top do not tarry long; the view is magnificent, but the wind is cold. Overcoats and wraps were brought along and they are needed; the thermometer registered eleven last night, and now it stands at thirty-three. It is a bleak, barren, wind-swept place, and yet it is healthy.

A family has been living here for five years. The husband and father is employed on the road and the mother has charge of the station. She has never been absent from the place, she says, since they took up their residence here. The oldest child was an infant when they came, and two have been born since. They are fine, healthy children, and have never been sick. A doctor has never visited them, she says, because one has never been needed. We are ready to leave before the train is ready to take us; a short visit to a place like this is sufficient. Several of the "boys" amuse themselves by snowballing one another and washing with snow the faces of some of the "girls."

Marshall Pass is 10,852 feet above the level of the sea, and is situated upon a point of the Great Continental Divide—on the ridge pole, as it were, between the Atlantic and Pacific slopes. Within the dingy snow shed where our train is standing we notice water slowly trickling down the bank into the ditch along the track; it makes a tiny stream, just large enough to flow, and we can see that it is running in each direction. A number of us place our fingers upon the dividing line, thus literally touching a point of the very comb of the great water shed between the Atlantic and Pacific Oceans.

Our return is made with more speed than our ascent, but in a very careful manner; helper engine 400 is detached and sent ahead. The descent is made by gravity, the air brakes being used to keep the train under control. Engineer Roney deserves great credit for the careful manner in which he handles the train. A stop of five minutes is made at Mear's Junction, where we make the acquaintance of Station Agent Smith, who, along with his duties as station agent and telegraph operator, is an artist of merit; a number of pictures of mountain scenery that he has painted adorn the walls of the station rooms.

When we get back to Salida and to our train it is 2.05 P. M. Eastern (12.05 P. M. Mountain) time. We find our friend McDonald looking for us, with an abundant lunch prepared, which we heartily appreciate and thoroughly enjoy. We are scheduled to leave here at one o'clock, and as it is nearing that time, we bid adieu to the good people of Salida who have shown us such a royal time, and at one o'clock, sharp, we steam away from the pretty little town, bound for Colorado Springs, 142 miles nearer home.

Leaving Salida we have engine 509, in charge of Engineer John Carr and Fireman R. Wilmonger. Our conductor is J. E. Duey, a member of Arkansas Valley Division No. 36, of Pueblo, Col. Brother Duey enjoys the notoriety of being a cousin to the late Jesse James, the famous bandit and train robber. The brakemen are S. G. Carlisle and William Shoemaker. Charlie Hooper is still with us, and at present is busily engaged in distributing fine photographic pictures of scenes along the picturesque Denver and Rio Grande Railroad. Mr. Hooper's kindness and generosity are greatly appreciated, and the pictures will be highly prized as valuable souvenirs of our trip. In addition to Mr. Hooper we have with us as guests Brothers W. Newman and Frank Smith, of Division 44, and Harry Hart, of Division 36. A short stop is made at Parkdale, 46 miles from Salida, where we meet Rev. John Brunton, who is invited to accompany us to Pueblo. Mr. Brunton, who is an old engineer, retired from active service, is First Division Chaplain, and has charge of the employés' reading room in Pueblo. He is an entertaining old gentleman; says he is employed to fight the devil, who is always sneaking around after railroad men. Brother Houston says, "A man like that is needed on the Schuylkill Division." No one replies to this insinuation, except Brother Reagan, who merely says, "Sure."

Soon after leaving Parkdale we enter the Grand Cañon of the Arkansas, which is 8 miles in length and the crowning wonder of all the marvelous sights we have yet beheld; a mighty pathway, right through the heart of the Rocky Mountains, hewn by Nature through inaccessible towering mountain walls. Through this narrow gorge, whose perpendicular walls rise to the height of over 2000 feet, the crowded, pent-up waters of the Arkansas River rush and roar and foam. There is scarcely space for both railroad and river, but with an audacity that knows no shrinking the intrepid engineers entered the walled-up, darksome cañon, and, following the intricate winding of the surging stream, laid their tracks of steel along its foam-flecked bank. Beyond a doubt it is the most daring feat of railroad engineering ever performed. When half way through the awful Royal Gorge is reached, here the river holds despotic, undisputed sway for a distance of 100 feet. There is no bank to lay the tracks upon; from wall to wall the river surges, leaps, and roars. From out the water those mighty walls, built by Nature's hand, run right straight up, 2600 feet in the air. Ingenuity and nerve solves the problem; a bridge is built parallel with the river's course, one side resting upon a granite ledge, hewn in the side of the cliff, the other side suspended from rods attached to the overhanging wall of the opposite cliff. Over this construction the trains securely pass, while underneath the torrent rushes on.

Before reaching the bridge our train stops, and as many as wish get out and walk over, in order to obtain a good view of the awe-inspiring grandeur of the Royal Gorge. It is truly a wonderful sight, and one we will never forget. We do not tarry long to contemplate the scenery, for a mean, commonplace shower of rain is falling, and we hurry to the train to avoid getting wet.

Issuing from the cañon, we enter a broad and fertile valley, through which flows the ever-present Arkansas River, and in a short time pass through Cañon City, a town of considerable importance, having a population of 3000, and the county seat of Fremont County. The State penitentiary is located here, and near by are mineral springs of great value, making it a favorite resort

THE ROYAL GORGE AND HANGING BRIDGE, GRAND CAÑON OF THE ARKANSAS.

for those in quest of retirement or health. We didn't stop. The sight of the broad, unfettered freedom of the fertile Arkansas Valley, with its hundreds of acres of fine orchards and miles of magnificent grazing land, is a pleasure and relief after so much cramped and rocky glory, and gloomy, walled-up grandeur.

Pueblo is reached at 6.25 P. M. Eastern (4.25 P. M. Mountain) time, and a stop of ten minutes is made for the purpose of changing engines. We have not time to take in the city, but we disembark and take a look about the depot, which is called Union Station, being the joint property of five different roads and used by them all, namely, the Denver and Rio Grande, Santa Fé, Missouri Pacific, Rock Island, and Union Pacific, Denver and Gulf. The building is composed of red sandstone, a handsome structure, and is commodious and convenient. Pueblo, though situated in a valley or basin surrounded on three sides by distant mountain ranges, enjoys an elevation of 4668 feet. It has a population of 40,000 inhabitants, is the centre of extensive mining industries and immense railroad traffic. Because of its great, ever-smoking smelters, and glowing furnaces and foundries, Pueblo is often called the "Pittsburgh of the West." The Arkansas River flows through the heart of the city, but is not navigable, and its sloping banks are neatly walled to prevent overflow in time of freshet. Bidding good-bye to our old new-found friend, Rev. Brunton, and waving adieu to the 509 and the gallant men in her cab who brought us safely through such scenes of weird, bewildering, perilous grandeur, we start on our way again with engine 534, in charge of Engineer Henry Hinman and Fireman George Courtly. Conductor Duey and Brakemen Carlisle and Shoemaker go with us to Colorado Springs.

After leaving Pueblo we pass through an extensive oil district, where many wells are in operation, and we are told the yield is very heavy. We arrive in Colorado Springs at 8.20 P. M. Eastern (6.20 P. M. Mountain) time, and escorted by Brothers Newman, Hart, Smith, and Mr. Hooper, we start out to see the town. Colorado Springs is a model town. It is quiet, clean, and dry; in fact, it is *very dry*, being entirely and teetotally temperance. But this is a commendable trait; we find no fault, and are all impressed with the morality and good order which prevail. It is a healthy place; the houses are not crowded together. The population is 12,000; the town has an elevation of 5982 feet, and covers an area of four square miles. It is much resorted to by invalids, and thousands, we are told, are yearly benefited by taking advantage of its exhilarating atmosphere, favorable climatic conditions, and the pleasure and enjoyment derived from interesting and beautiful natural environments.

Soon after starting out we encounter Brother D. F. McPherson, secretary and treasurer of Holy Cross Division 252, of Leadville, who joins us in our rambles. After giving the quiet little city a pretty thorough inspection, we are grouped upon a corner discussing where we shall go next. "We have shown you the most cleanly and orderly town in the State of Colorado," remarks Mr. Hooper, "and now I would like to show you just the reverse; we will take the next car and slip over to Oldtown." In two minutes the car comes, and getting aboard, a ride of two miles brings us to the neigh-

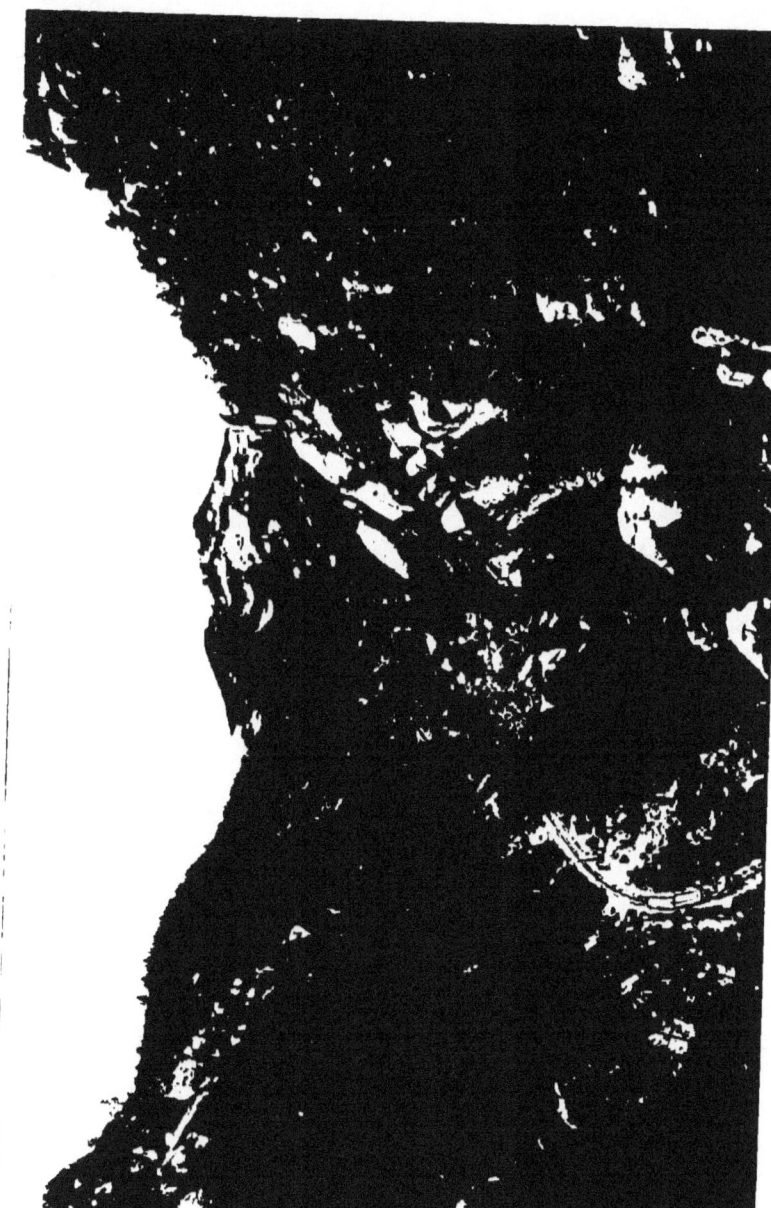

ASCENT OF PIKE'S PEAK BY MANITOU AND PIKE'S PEAK RAILROAD (COG WHEEL)

boring town, where it seems every third door is a saloon and gambling resort. Wherever we go there is turmoil and excitement. We see no outbreaks of strife, but in these crowded gambling rooms we visit, the swarthy miner and reckless stockman jostle one another in their eagerness to reach the tempting roulette wheel or alluring faro table. We can see they are excited, although they are calm, but it is the calmness of suppressed emotion, and we are careful as we move among them not to tread upon their toes; not that we are afraid to tramp their toes if we want to, but we don't want to; we didn't come out West to make trouble, so we are always careful what we do, if we are not so careful where we go.

Getting enough of Oldtown, we board a car and are soon back in sedate Colorado Springs and seek our train, that is sidetracked for occupancy near the station. I size up the crowd as they file in and find some are missing; they have dropped out of the ranks and escaped us, and—more "unwritten history." It is near midnight, all is dark and silent, and we quietly seek our berths.

## WEDNESDAY, JUNE 2d.

All are up about the usual time this morning, and after breakfast Manager Wyman announces that those who wish to make the ascent of Pike's Peak will take the 8.30 train on the Colorado Springs and Manitou Branch for Manitou, six miles away, where the Manitou and Pike's Peak railway station is located. The 8.30 train starts with about half of our party on board. It is cloudy and we are afraid the weather will be unfavorable for the trip. When we arrive at the station in Manitou we can see that the great mountain is enveloped in fog and mist. We hesitate about going up, but the station agent receives a telephone message from the summit, saying the weather up there is clear, and the most of us decide to go. And when at 9.40 we start, I notice the occupants of the car and find the following members of our party aboard: Mr. and Mrs. Wyman, Mr. and Mrs. Maxwell, Mr. and Mrs. Layfield, Mr. and Mrs. Horner, Mr. and Mrs. Mitchell, Mr. and Mrs. Smith, Mr. and Mrs. Dougherty, Mr. and Mrs. Climenson, Mr. and Mrs. Foulon, Mr. and Mrs. Elder, Mr. and Mrs. Reilly, Mr. and Miss Barrett and a lady friend, Miss Emma Leibing; Mr. Reagan and a lady friend, Miss Jennie Heaney; Mrs. Mattson, Messrs. Waddington, Haas, Taylor, Crispen, Denniston, Moore, Williams, Sloane, Kilgore, Restein, and myself. The car is pushed by engine No. 4, in charge of Engineer D. M. Jones. This little locomotive is an odd-looking thing, built expressly for this line by the Baldwin Locomotive Works, of Philadelphia, Pa. It has four cylinders and carries 200 pounds steam pressure. It is constructed with two cog wheels underneath its centre, which operate in corresponding cog rails placed in the centre of the track, and has the appearance of being a strong and safe appliance. Engine and car are not coupled together, but the engine in the rear pushes the car ahead of it, which gives the tourist a fine, unobstructed view of the scenery.

The grade averages almost 900 feet to the mile, which we ascend at the rate of about five miles per hour. The road is almost nine miles in length and we are one hour and forty-five minutes making the ascent, having left

GATEWAY TO THE GARDEN OF THE GODS, COLORADO; PIKE'S PEAK IN THE DISTANCE.

the station at Manitou at 9.40 and arriving at the summit at 11.25. We thought it was a slow trip and a tedious climb, but it wasn't when we consider the experience of some other people in connection with this mountain several years ago. Ambition and desire are strong impulses in human nature, often having more influence than a sense of duty.

When Major Zebulon M. Pike first sighted this mountain that bears his name on the morning of November 13th, 1806, he had a burning desire to give it a close inspection, and led his followers a ten days' rugged march before he reached its base. From this point he looked up to its apparently inaccessible snow-crowned summit, and concluded it would be impossible to scale its rocky, bouldered sides. Retiring from the locality, he reported that he "had discovered a grand mountain peak, bare of vegetation and covered with snow, but he believed that no human being could ever ascend to its pinnacle."

When, thirteen years afterwards, on the morning of July 13th, 1819, Dr. Edwin James and his four comrades stood and gazed upon the terribly wild and awful grandeur of this mighty mountain peak, they faced the same conditions that caused the intrepid Pike to turn his back upon the scene and withdraw: perpendicular cliffs whose walls no man can climb, enormous rocks and giant boulders impossible to remove or surmount, great chasms that cannot be crossed or bridged, deep, wild ravines that seem to be impenetrable. All this they saw, yet they did not hesitate, for they were filled with a wild ambition and burning desire to accomplish what Pike had not dared to undertake. So they started, and after two days of perilous hardship and toil they reached the summit, on July 14th, 1819.

Their ambition was gratified, and so is ours. We did not come up for pleasure, for there is no pleasure in it; the novelty of the thing brought us here, and we find it novel enough. We wanted to stand on the apex of these snow-bound, wind-swept, zero-blistered heights, 14,147 feet above the beating billows of the sea, and see what it is like. We are finding out; it is colder than Chestnut Hill in midwinter. The snow is six feet deep and the wind whistles a tune as it sweeps through Colonel Layfield's whiskers. The sun is shining when we get out of the car, and with the snow whirling down our backs and tears streaming from our eyes we spend three minutes looking down upon the far-away valley scenery and the towns of Manitou and Colorado Springs. Then we enter the old Government signal station, which has been turned into a curio shop, telegraph office, post office, and restaurant. We find the temperature more congenial, and put in the time examining and purchasing novelties which are neither valuable or cheap, but are wanted for souvenirs. We buy postal cards at ten cents each and mail them to friends, and send telegrams at five cents per word. Manager Wyman sends a dispatch to Ticket Receiver Stackhouse, Philadelphia, informing him of our whereabouts and condition, but he couldn't tell it all. The message didn't tell how near Waddie was to being fired off the train at Hell Gate because he couldn't find his ticket, as Restein had it in his pocket; nor how eager Sloane was to chase the badger we saw running over the rocks above Timber Line, but the conductor wouldn't stop the train to let him off.

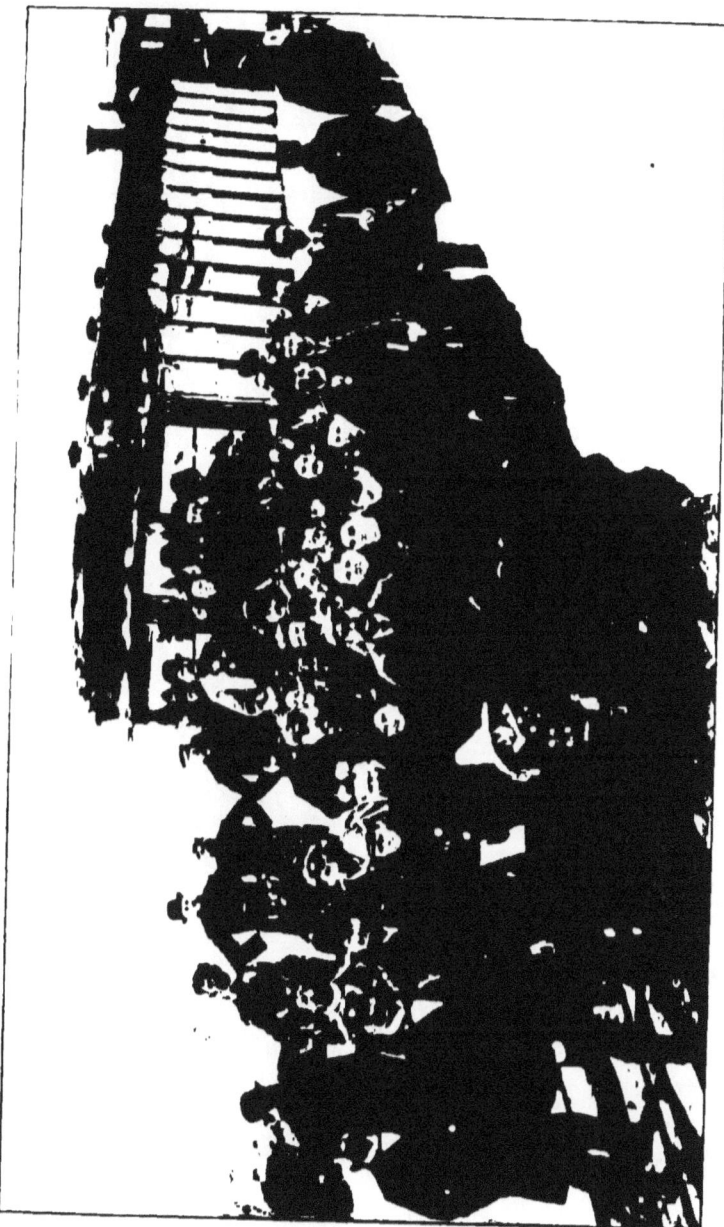

ON PIKE'S PEAK: ALTITUDE 14,147 FEET.

We have got enough of Pike's Peak and are ready to go, but the engine is away with the snow plow and we will have to wait for its return. We have seen all there is to be seen and have bought what souvenirs we want. My last purchase was a tissue-paper napkin; I gave thirty cents for it, but had a cup of coffee and a sandwich thrown in. Our engine has returned and we go out to get in the car. The sun is hidden by a great dark cloud, the wind blows harder than ever, and the car is locked up. A photographer is on hand with his outfit and wants to take a picture; somebody ought to throw him over the precipice. We are huddled about the end of the car like a tempest-stricken flock outside a sheepfold gate, shivering and shaking in the blast. As the picture fiend adjusts the camera it begins to snow; in thirty seconds we are in a raging blizzard, the instrument snaps and the car door is unlocked, but before we all get inside many of us are covered with snow.

We are in the storm until we get below Timber Line, and the force of the wind drives the snow across the car as it sifts through the ventilators and in around the windows, and some of us are feeling pretty groggy. I do not like the sensation; when I speak I talk through my hat, and my ear drums feel ready to burst. When I go up so high again I want to go to stay; there may be such a thing as becoming acclimated.

The descent is made in a careful manner, with the engine in front. We arrive safely in Manitou at 1.40 P. M., and the party scatters. Some return to Colorado Springs and some drive through the Garden of the Gods. Many who did not ascend the peak have had a good time visiting other interesting places, and tell interesting stories of the remarkable things they saw. The little burros or donkeys are in evidence everywhere, and several of our people got their photos taken seated on these cute little animals with the Balance Rock in the background. Some of the timid ladies of our party, I am told, are shy of these meek little creatures, saying they look fierce and dangerous because their ears are so large. The only danger is in their hind feet, for they can kick very quick and hard, injuring one another sometimes in this way when they get to frolicking, which they often do.

Brother Schuler was in one of the carriages that drove through the "Garden of the Gods" to-day, and it is interesting to hear him relate in his inimitable manner the many curious things to be seen. A heavy thunder and hail storm descended upon Manitou this afternoon, with another blizzard on the peak, and the weather has become quite cool. Mrs. E. T. Postlewaite took dinner with us to-day as a guest of Brother and Mrs. Springer. Our people are scattered this evening, amusing themselves in various ways. Brothers Brown, Horner, and myself take a stroll after dinner. We stop at the Antlers Hotel, that is well worth a visit, being one of the finest-equipped hotels we have seen in our travels.

We were introduced to the chief of police of the city and kindly shown the large, interesting, and gruesome collection in the Rogues' Gallery, pictures of some of the most noted crooks and renegades that ever infested the West, along with weapons and tools of all descriptions that were used in their murderous and nefarious business. One set of burglar implements, in particular, containing one hundred and fifty-five pieces, that had been

BRIDE AND GROOM AT BALANCE ROCK, GARDEN OF THE GODS, COLORADO.

captured from a suspect by the name of Jerome Markle, we find very interesting; it is said to be the largest and most complete burglar's outfit ever captured. Returning to the train about 9.30, we are glad to meet W. E. Frenaye, Esq., city editor of the Colorado Springs *Gazette*, who has dropped in on us for a friendly chat. Mr. Frenaye was connected with Assistant General Passenger Agent Boyd's office at one time, and is an old friend of Brother Maxwell. Being scheduled to leave here at 2 o'clock A. M., we all turn in at a reasonable hour.

## THURSDAY, JUNE 3d.

Getting up this morning at six o'clock, I find we are entering Denver. We have engine 570, Engineer Wm. Jenness, Fireman W. C. Lawhead, Conductor I. Larsen, Brakemen Cunningforth and McGinn. Soon as the train stops, Mrs. Terry and Mrs. Shaw strike off in search of the post office, for they are expecting letters from home. Our train is sidetracked in the yard and Brother Terry and I walk over to the station, a short distance away, and look around. It is pretty quiet; the great city has not wakened up to the business of the day and the railroads haven't commenced their bustle and confusion. This is a large station, one of the finest we have seen in the West; twelve railroads use it, which diverge from here in all directions and run to all parts of the United States. This is what a railroad time table tells us that I have just picked up. It also tells us that Denver is considerable of a town, that it is the county seat of Arapahoe County and the capital of the State of Colorado. It enjoys an altitude of 5196 feet and has a population of 165,000 inhabitants.

We return to the train and find breakfast waiting. While we are at breakfast the ladies return from the post office; they were too early to get letters, for the office wasn't open, but they were loaded with souvenirs they had procured on the way. After breakfast we are notified to remove all stuff from our sections to the baggage car, as the cars are to be cleaned. This is a notice that isn't calculated to sweeten temper. It has been served on us several times since we started from home, and we know what an annoyance it is, but we rejoice to know this is the last time we will suffer the inconvenience.

After this task is accomplished a number of us take a 25-mile ride around the city on the "Seeing Denver" trolley line. It is a delightful ride, and in this way we see many interesting features of the "Queen City of the Plains." The car we are on is No. 111, in charge of Motorman Ewell and Conductor F. F. Porter. Mr. H. Given accompanies the car and points out and explains interesting localities and places. We can see that the educational facilities of Denver are up to date. Our attention is called to Westminster University, located on a knoll just beyond the city limits, said to be one of the finest institutions of learning in the State. We pass near the Louisa M. Alcott Public School, one of the finest public buildings we have ever seen. Having reached the suburbs we are out amongst cultivated fields, and Mr. Given, in speaking of the fertility of Colorado soil and the abundance of their crops, called our attention to the rich growth of the alfalfa grass in a field close at hand. At the utterance of the word *alfalfa* a protest went up from the party; they had had all the alfalfa they wanted in Texas, and begged Mr. Given to give them no

MANITOU SPRINGS, COLORADO.

more. Manager Wyman explained why our people dislike the name of alfalfa. Mr. Given said he could but acknowledge that we had just reasons to boycott the name, and thought he could give us some information that would increase our dislike the more. "Perhaps you do not know," he continues, "that there are hundreds of tons of alfalfa leaves shipped yearly from Colorado to New York to adulterate the tea you drink?" This is certainly news to us; it is something we did not know, nor are we sure of it yet, notwithstanding Mr. Given's assertion; nevertheless it may be true.

We cross the South Fork of the Platte River, that flows through the centre of the town, from which the city's supply of water is taken, and are shown the Public Park, containing four hundred acres, that is kept up by a tax on the city property owners amounting to $125,000 a year. Our attention is directed to the towering smokestack of the Omaha and Giant Smelter, which rises to the height of 352 feet and is said to be the highest chimney in the world. This is one of the most extensive smelters in America, and since its erection, a trifle over twelve years ago, it has treated ore amounting to nearly $300,000,000. In addition to the Omaha and Giant Smelter there are a number of other plants in active operation. The ores treated are gold, silver, copper, and lead. The total product of the Denver smelting industry amounts to $40,000,000 per year.

Denver is six by ten miles in extent, and I think we rode all the way around it and part way through it. It is a city of beautiful, substantial residences and superb public buildings, the most noticeable being the State Capitol Building, completed in 1895 and costing $2,-550,000.

The streets of this great city are not in as clean a condition as they might be; mud in many places is ankle deep, caused, Mr. Given informs us, by the recent heavy rains turning the dust into mud. What an awful dusty city it must be when not muddy; we imagine an occasional heavy shower is a great relief, for dust is a far greater evil than mud. We would quietly suggest to the City Fathers of this great metropolis, for the sake of the health and comfort of their citizens and the pleasure and convenience of visitors, that they eliminate the dust from their town by scraping up and carting to the dump the mud from the streets, through which pedestrians are forced to wade every time it rains.

Our trolley ride finished, we alight at Brown's Palace Hotel. This magnificent structure, covering an entire block, ten stories in height, built of brown sandstone, interior finished in Mexican onyx, and costing the neat little sum of $2,000,000, is the pride of Denver. Here "The H. J. Mayham Investment Company" has its headquarters in a suite of offices on the first floor. We are kindly received by Mr. W. H. Coombs, a representative of the company, who loads us down with illustrated and descriptive books and pamphlets.

It is now past noon, and from here our party scatters. Mrs. Shaw desires to visit Mrs. Edward Bicking, formerly Miss Madeline Ramsey, of West Chester, Pa., who is living in or near Denver. We consult a directory that gives Mr. Bicking's address as 313 Ashland Avenue, Highlands. We immediately take a car, and after a lengthy ride arrive at the given address only to find they had moved to Golden, 15 miles west of Denver. Returning to the Union Depot, we take the 3.10 train on the Union Pacific, Denver and Gulf Railway, and arrive in Golden after a pleasant ride of forty-five minutes. We have no difficulty in finding the pleasant home of Mr. Bicking, where we meet with a cordial welcome. They persuade us to remain over night with them and we enjoy our visit very much. Mr. Bicking operates a large paper mill, and having no competition does a large and thriving business. Golden is a pleasant, healthy town, having an elevation of 5655 feet. It has about 3000 population and until 1868 was the capital of Colorado. It is situated on Clear Creek, a fine mountain stream, and near the entrance to the famous Clear Creek Cañon. It is surrounded by towering cliffs and great mountain ranges, amongst which it quietly nestles.

Years ago Golden was a stirring mining camp, but the excitement and bustle of the mining industry has been moved farther up the cañon, leaving this community in comparative quiet. Last July a cloudburst occurred in the mountains, and the flood, rushing down the cañon, swept through the town of Golden, destroying much property and drowning several persons. We took a walk in the evening with Mr. and Mrs. Bicking around the town and saw many traces of the awfully destructive deluge.

I learned before leaving Denver this afternoon that a trip for to-morrow had been planned for our party, over the Union Pacific, Denver and Gulf Railway, up Clear Creek Cañon to Silver Plume, 54 miles from Denver. The train is due in Golden at nine o'clock. It is our purpose to meet it and join the party. Having spent a very pleasant afternoon and evening, we retired about ten o'clock.

## FRIDAY, JUNE 4th.

Having enjoyed a good night's rest, we arose about seven o'clock, and after breakfast Mr. Bicking escorted us over his mill, which is only a short distance from the pleasant cottage in which they reside. The time arriving for us to start for the station, we bid adieu to our kind friends and join our party on the train under the escort of F. M. Shaw, traveling agent of the Union Pacific, Denver and Gulf Railway, bound for Silver Plume, up the picturesque Clear Creek Cañon, and over the Great Loop. We have U. P. D. & G. Ry. engine No. 7, with Engineer Si Allen at the throttle. The train is in charge of Conductor John W. Ryan, a member of Denver Division 44, who is an old friend of Brother Reagan's. The two had not met for years, and the reunion was a happy one. It was through the efforts of Conductor Ryan that we are given this pleasant trip to-day.

Leaving Golden, we enter the wilds of Clear Creek Cañon, similar in many respects to Eagle River Cañon, the mighty sloping hills on either side being honeycombed with mines. In places the cañon is very narrow; the rugged walls overhanging the tracks almost meet at the top, a thousand feet above. The stream we follow is a shallow one, and here and there we catch sight of a prospector wading in the water with his shovel and pan, washing the sand he scoops up from the bottom of the creek in the hope of finding grains of gold. A diligent prospector, we are told, realizes in this manner from two to ten dollars per day. For 22 miles we follow the windings of Clear Creek up through this narrow, rocky gorge, and then the cañon terminates in an open, level

BACHELORS AND BURROS IN THE GARDEN OF THE GODS.

plateau of about one hundred acres, surrounded by seamed and rugged mountains, grinning with prospectors' pits and the open mouths of mines.

Here is located the pretty little mining town of Idaho Springs, at an elevation of 7543 feet. We make a stop of ten minutes and get out to look around. We run right along the edge of the creek and several of the boys look for gold in the sand of the shallow water, but I hear of none being found. It is cloudy, a light rain is falling, and having reached a pretty high altitude the wind is chilly. Leaving Idaho Springs the open observation car is almost deserted, the closed coaches being far more comfortable, the most of our people caring more for comfort than for scenery. Thirteen miles from Idaho Springs we pass through Georgetown, a mining town of considerable size. Here we commence the Great Loop ascension; the railway winding around the mountain crosses itself at one point, and looking down we see nearly 200 feet beneath us the track where we had been but a short time before. Thus we climb until we reach Silver Plume, at an elevation of 9176 feet, arriving there at 12.20 Mountain time.

Leaving the train, we visit the Victoria Tunnel and Mendota Mine. Under the escort of the mine boss the majority of the party enter the mine, each one bearing a lighted candle, for the tunnel is dark as a dungeon. This tunnel is hewn from the solid rock and extends for 2000 feet straight into the mountain side before the rich vein of silver ore is reached. When we reach the end of the tunnel we are almost directly under the centre of the peak, a thousand feet under the surface of the ground. After procuring a few small pieces of ore as souvenirs we retraced our steps and were glad to get out into open daylight once more. On our return to the train we encountered a light snow squall. We leave Silver Plume at 2.15 o'clock for return trip, with Brothers Maxwell, Reagan, and Agent Shaw on the cowcatcher. A donkey on the track sees us coming, flops his left ear, switches his tail, and wisely steps aside. We arrive safely in Denver at six o'clock and find dinner waiting in our dining car, to which we all ably respond, feeling that in McDonald and his worthy attachés we have valued friends. After dinner our people scattered over the city, amusing themselves in various ways, and not having furnished the writer with reports of their experience, he can but note, "unwritten history."

Brother F. H. Conboy, of Division 44, has kindly made arrangements with the managers of the Overland Park races to admit members of our party at reduced rates, and a number talk of attending the races to-morrow should the weather prove favorable. We are not very highly impressed with this climate at the present time, for it is entirely too cold and damp to be agreeable.

## SATURDAY, JUNE 5th.

According to our original itinerary this is the day we should arrive in Philadelphia, yet here we are at Denver, in the midst of as disagreeable a spell of weather, we are told, as ever was known here. Each afternoon since we have been here it has snowed on the mountains and rained in the valleys; heavy wraps and overcoats are worn by our people when they venture away from the train. "This is not a sample of Colorado weather," I hear Charlie

Hooper declare, and we are all very glad it isn't, for the sake of the people who have to stay here; we are not going to remain much longer, and wouldn't be here now, only for the irrepressible tantrums of the Rio Grande River. Our people scatter again to-day, and I cannot tell where they went or what they saw.

Mrs. Shaw and myself visited an old friend and former neighbor, David Cannon, on his beautiful Broadway dairy ranch, six miles south of Denver. An electric line runs within half a mile of his residence. We were very cordially received and spent a pleasant day. We also visited the splendid Windsor ranch, owned by Major Dubois, ex-mayor of Leadville, and operated by Messrs. Penrose and Cannon. We met the Major and Miss Dubois and were very kindly treated by them. The Windsor and Broadway dairy farms comprise a fine, beautiful, level tract of land, containing 1000 acres in a highly improved condition. It commenced to rain again about three o'clock and we returned to the city in a cold, beating storm. Mrs. Bicking, who was with us, remarked that in the four years of her residence in Colorado she had, heretofore, experienced no such weather as this.

The rain had ceased when we reached our train, about five o'clock. Found most of our company there and photo artists Stanton and Warren with their outfit, preparing to picture the train and party. We forthwith arrange ourselves in a group about the end of the train in a manner according to the instructions of the artists. Mrs. Bicking is requested to join the group and her little son, Austin, is placed upon the platform of the car. Our dinner this evening was an interesting and happy occasion. Brother Reagan's friend, Conductor John Ryan, and his family were guests, and during the repast Mr. Ryan presented Brother Reagan with a handsome floral tribute, representing a keystone, composed of roses and carnations, with inscription in immortelles: "From Jack to John, who were Boys Together." Below the inscription, artistically wrought with the same kind of flowers, is a representation of clasped hands. Brothers Reagan and Ryan were boys together, grew up and learned railroading together, but have been separated for about eighteen years. The event was a happy one and will be long remembered by those who participated. A few of our people attended the Overland Park races to-day, but the weather was unfavorable for the sport. Brother Crispin met an old schoolmate this afternoon, Mr. J. H. Harris, who is connected with the inspection department of the Denver and Rio Grande Road. Mr. Harris took charge of Brother Crispin and several others and showed them a good time.

We are scheduled to leave here at midnight, and conclude to remain up till we start. There is usually an entertaining time in the smoker and the hours pass quickly away. We start promptly at 2.01 A. M. Eastern (12.01 A. M. Mountain) time over the Burlington and Missouri River Railroad, known as the "Burlington Route," with B. & M. engine 317, Engineer W. Fuller, Fireman C. Babcock, Conductor C. W. Bronson, Brakeman E. Q. Robie. As guests we have with us leaving Denver Trainmaster J. F. Kenyon and Traveling Engineer C. A. Dickson. It is now past midnight; we have said goodbye to the kind friends who remained with us till the start, and as we leave the great city of Denver behind us we feel both glad and sorry; glad that we are once more speeding toward our Eastern homes, but sorry to lose sight of the matchless Colorado scenery and part with our kind and generous Colorado friends. The efforts made to show us a good time by the kind people of Denver and by the railway officials of the various lines are highly appreciated by each member of the party. Charlie Hooper will be remembered so long as memory of the trip shall last; may his appetite never grow less nor his shadow ever shrink.

## SUNDAY, JUNE 6th.

Got up this morning about seven o'clock and found we were approaching McCook, Neb., having crossed the line from Colorado into Nebraska during the night at a point about 80 miles west of McCook. Conductor Bronson and Brakeman Robie are members of Harvey Division No. 95, of McCook. They have intimated that we may expect a reception from the members of that division on our arrival at McCook; this information having been given out last evening, the most of our people are up when the train stops in McCook at ten minutes past seven, and we are met by a large delegation of brothers of Division 95 with their wives and daughters, who give us a cordial, happy greeting. The McCook Band is on hand and renders delightful music, and the hour allowed us here passes quickly away. B. & M. engine 232, in charge of Engineer J. E. Sanborn and fired by Charlie Williams, has been selected to draw us from McCook to Hastings, a distance of 132 miles. Engineer Sanborn is a member of Harvey Division 95, having at one time been a conductor, and has the 232 handsomely decorated with flags and flowers in honor of the occasion. On each side of the cab beneath the windows are the letters "O. R. C.," surrounded by the emblem of the order. The engine is much admired by the members of our party, and snap-shots are taken by Brothers Restein and Foster.

Left McCook at 10.00 Eastern (9.00 Central) time. On leaving McCook time changes from Mountain to Central, and we now run one hour behind Eastern time. From McCook to Hastings we have with us as guests Brothers V. H. Halliday, F. Kendler, and C. E. Pope, who are members of the entertainment committee from Division 95, and the following ladies of McCook: Mrs. C. W. Bronson, Mrs. V. H. Halliday, Mrs. F. Kendler, Mrs. C. E. Pope, Mrs. Beyer, Miss Grace Sanborn, and Miss Mabel Jordon. We have a pleasant entertainment in the combined car, during which Mrs. Bronson and Miss Sanborn sing in a charming manner several choice selections. Arriving in Hastings at twelve o'clock, noon, we make a halt of five minutes to change engines, and bidding adieu to the kind friends of McCook who gave us such a royal greeting, we continue on our way with engine 227, Engineer H. L. Beaty, Fireman F. C. Parkerson, Conductor J. G. Chase, Brakeman Fred. Sharpe. Our guests are Brothers M. E. Shepard, of Claude Champion Division No. 227, of Lincoln, Neb., M. E. Crane, of Creston Division No. 21, of Creston, Iowa, and Trainmaster E. W. Carter.

At Fairmount, 43 miles from Hastings, we make a short stop to allow some guests to get aboard; they are Brothers W. B. Morledge, J. H. Burns, of Division 227,

"WHO ARE WE? WHO ARE WE? P. P. C.! COOKS, WAITERS, AND PORTERS OF THE O. R. C.!"

THE "232." McCOOK, NEBRASKA.

W. J. Robinson, of Omaha Division 126, and Chief Dispatcher C. L. Eaton. Brother Burns is entitled to special mention, being introduced to us as "the largest conductor on the Burlington Route. He is 6 feet 1 inch tall and weighs 290 pounds." "If we only had 'Big Frank,' of the New York Division, with us," says Brother Denniston, "we could beat that by 1 inch and 10 pounds."

"While we are not able to produce our largest conductor to compare him with yours," spoke up Manager Wyman, "we have with us one who enjoys the distinction of being the smallest conductor on the Pennsylvania Railroad System, being but 5 feet 3 inches in height and weighing only 109 pounds. I take pleasure in introducing you to Brother Charles L. Springer." Brother Springer took the joke good-naturedly and responds in a pleasant manner, telling the advantage of being small; that his size enables him to get through places with ease where large men dare not attempt to go. We notice that Conductor Chase is a great favorite with the ladies of our party, who are trying to rob his uniform coat of its pretty golden buttons, that they covet for souvenirs. A stop of half an hour is made at Lincoln, where we arrive at three o'clock. Conductor Chase, to save his coat, procures a number of uniform buttons and distributes them among the ladies. Division 227 adjourned meeting this afternoon to meet us at the station on our arrival, an action very much appreciated by our boys, and the half hour was spent in pleasant greetings. The "boys," the cooks, waiters, and porters, and the ladies gave their yells in turn as the time came for us to leave, and the effort of the ladies was loudly applauded.

We leave Lincoln with the same engine and crew that brought us from Hastings, and they take us to Pacific Junction, a run of 177 miles. We feel that we are in good hands, for Conductor J. G. Chase was selected to take charge, from Pacific Junction to Hastings, of the Mayham Special, that on February 15th and 16th, 1897, broke the world's record for long-distance running, having made the run from Chicago to Denver, a distance of 1025 miles, in 1047 minutes. Engine 227 that is now pulling us drew the special from Lincoln to Hastings, a distance of 96 miles, in 109 minutes, a speed of about 53 miles per hour. This did not quite reach the average rate of speed made on the trip, which was 58¾ miles per hour. Leaving Lincoln we have with us as additional guests Brothers W. C. McDermott and C. Kast, of Division 227, and Engineer F. B. Arnold. We arrive in Omaha at 5.15 P. M., and within ten minutes after our arrival we are speeding through the city on electric cars, under the escort of Brother W. J. Robinson and Superintendent of Street Car Service T. H. Todhunter, who has placed two fine open trolley cars at our service and personally directs their movements, switching us from one thoroughfare to another until almost the entire city is traversed. It is a pleasant afternoon and we greatly enjoy the delightful ride through this, one of the greatest cities of the West, noted for its rapid growth, having increased from a population of 30,518 in 1880 to 140,452 in 1890, and we are told that present indications point to the likelihood of it reaching 300,000 in time for the census of 1900.

Omaha is up to date in all that pertains to the health, comfort, and welfare of her citizens, and we are all favorably impressed with her clean streets, pleasant homes, and fine, substantial public buildings. Omaha has a curfew law, recently established, the beneficent effects of which are already noticed and highly recommended. It keeps off the streets after nine o'clock at night boys and girls under sixteen years of age, unless accompanied by parents or guardians.

We have consumed more time in doing the town of Omaha than was intended, and consequently, when we leave at 7.05 we are thirty-five minutes late on our schedule; but we are on a line noted for its "fast time," and probably the delay will be made up. A number of the boys from Creston Division No. 21 and their ladies came up to Omaha to meet us this afternoon, and return with us to Creston.

We have the pleasure of having with us L. H. Wright, C. C. of No. 21, Mr. and Mrs. R. McCoy, Mr. and Mrs. J. W. Smelley, Mr. and Mrs. J. C. Felker, Mr. and Mrs. Nugent, Mr. and Miss Bradey, Mr. Donoven, Train Dispatcher Ed. Robeson, Master Mechanic G. L. Beckwith, J. W. Fedder and mother, Mr. and Mrs. Roberts, F. M. Price, Miss Galeger, Miss Thompson, Miss Gaul, Miss Gaven, Miss Obine. Leaving Omaha we do not cross the Missouri River and enter Iowa via Council Bluffs, but follow the river south for 26 miles to Plattsmouth, where we cross the turbid stream on a substantial bridge and enter Iowa at Pacific Junction, having traversed the southern border of the State of Nebraska for 366 miles. We saw a fine, level country, dotted with neat, substantial farm buildings, and judging from the many well-filled cribs of last year's corn, it must be a country extremely rich in agricultural products.

At Pacific Junction a change of engines and crews is made, and bidding adieu to good-hearted, good-natured Captain Chase and his genial crew, we continue on our way with C. B. & Q. engine 318, in charge of Engineer George Goodrich and Fireman T. H. Hillis, conducted by M. Farrell, whose brakemen are T. A. McDonald and T. Munson, who will take us to Creston, a run of 86 miles. Thirty-five miles from Pacific Junction we make a short stop at Redwood, and receive additional guests in the persons of Division Superintendent J. H. Duggan, Mr. Frank Gillman, J. B. Kirsh, chief engineer of Creston Division No. 112, B. of L. E., and Conductor T. G. Snair. We have now about thirty-five guests aboard and our train is pretty well filled up. It seems to be an off Sunday with many of the good people along the line, and they have turned out to show us a good time, and they can never guess how much their efforts are appreciated. It is 10.15 P. M. when we arrive in Creston, and as we approach the station Superintendent Duggan, who has been watching the time, informs us that our train has covered the last 36 miles in forty-two minutes. A large bonfire is burning on an open lot near the station, and the juvenile band of Creston is playing a stirring piece when our train comes to a halt. There is a large crowd on hand to greet us, and the forty-five minutes we remain among them passes quickly and pleasantly away. We bid good-bye to our many new-found friends, and at 11.02 P. M. leave Creston with C. B. & Q. engine 232, with Engineer J. Consodine at the throttle, and conducted by G. W. Yetts. The brakemen are W. D. Willits and G. A. Bessey, which crew takes us to Burlington, 190 miles. The "232" was also on the famous

Mayham Special from Creston to Red Oak, and made a record of 62½ miles per hour. Conductor Yetts had charge of the train from Burlington to Creston.

We have had a full day, and every one of the party feels that we have been honored by the demonstrations of good-fellowship that have marked our progress through the States of Nebraska and Iowa. We are all very tired to-night; this is the thirtieth day of our outing; each day a picnic and every night a circus. It is now drawing near the midnight hour, and as we steam away from the hospitable, wide-awake little town of Creston, with her bonfire and her band, our sincere wish is that the sun of prosperity may ever shine upon her. The combined car has been vacated and the refreshment corner is deserted; George H. Anderson, the hardest-worked man in the outfit, is making up his bed, Brother Sparks' El Paso pup has ceased his whining and now is snoring, and Sister Matthews' Denver magpie for once in its life is silent. These things I notice as I quietly leave the smoker and make my way to little No. 3, in the "Marco."

## MONDAY, JUNE 7th.

Getting up this morning about six o'clock, I find we are in Illinois, having crossed the Mississippi River during the night at Burlington, where a change of engines was made. We now have C. B. & Q. engine 511, handled by Engineer D. Sullivan and fired by J. Watson. Conductor W. L. Boydston, a member of Galesburg Division No. 83, has charge of our train, whose brakemen are J. M. Forsythe and T. G. White. This engine and crew will run us to Chicago, a distance of 206 miles.

Illinois is a rich agricultural State, whose well-cultivated farms and fine buildings exhibit a high degree of prosperity and thrift. Arriving in Chicago at 8.45 our people scatter to take in the sights of the city as best suit their individual inclinations. I have no knowledge as to where they went or what they saw, but the inference is that everybody was busy, for it is a physical impossibility for a person to remain still in this town; such hustling, aggressive activity I never saw before. If you attempt to saunter or stop to look you are the victim of a hundred bumps a minute; you've got to get in the race and keep going, or climb a tree.

On our arrival Mrs. S. and I were met by Mrs. Ray Melchor, Mrs. Shaw's sister, a resident of the city, who took charge of us, and I am glad she assumed the responsibility, for I never felt more in need of a guardian in my life than I did when in the heart of this mighty metropolis with its great sky-scraping buildings and tearing cyclone of humanity. Mrs. Melchor proved an excellent guide, and showed us more of this wonderful town than one would think possible in the few hours allotted us, besides giving us a delightful carriage ride along the lake front and through Jackson and Washington Parks. We also visited Lincoln Park and saw the famous Ferris Wheel. Mrs. Melchor returned with us to the train and accompanied us as far as the suburban station of Englewood, where the train was stopped to allow her to alight. We left Chicago at 5.40 P. M. on the Pittsburgh, Fort Wayne and Chicago Line, with P. Ft. W. & C. engine 147, Engineer Frank Higgins, Fireman Robt. Giffin, Conductor M. J. Prindiville, Brakeman H. B. Walton, and Flagman Geo. Roberts, who take us to Ft. Wayne, 148 miles. Near Whiting, a short distance beyond the limits of Chicago, we cross the line and enter Indiana, which also has the appearance of being a rich agricultural State.

In the evening an interesting meeting is held in the smoking car, and presided over by Brother Geo. Brown, for the purpose of effecting a permanent club, to be composed of the members of the Pennsylvania Railroad conductors' excursion party. Selecting a name leads to considerable discussion, until Brother Denniston suggests the "Golden Gate Club," which is unanimously adopted. The following brothers are elected officers of the club: President, C. E. Wyman; vice-president, L. E. Sheppard; secretary and treasurer, W. J. Maxwell. Pullman conductors Suter and McDonald are admitted as honorary members. The meeting, which lasted from 8.30 to 9.20 P. M., is succeeded by the admission to the car of a delegation of the ladies, led by Sister Reilly, who introduces an entertaining game called "The California Pets," or "Dead Hand," which consists of an outstretched sheet, around which sit as many as can conveniently do so, with their hands beneath the sheet, and guess the names of articles that they cannot see, which are passed from one to the other. The game continues for some time and produces a great deal of merriment, until an article is passed to Miss Ella that causes her to shriek with fright. She quickly passes it to Brother Reagan, who turns pale and shudders as though he had seen a ghost; he in turn tosses it to Brother Williams, who is thrown into a spasm when he grasps the nasty thing, and flings it into Brother McCarty's lap, who clutches it, drops it, exclaims "Hell!" jumps up, all at the same time, and makes a break for the door. It was only a kid glove that Mrs. Reilly had filled with sand and soaked in ice water, that felt to the touch like the cold and clammy hand of a corpse.

The rear car "Orchis" was christened "Hogan's Alley" in the early stages of our trip, because of the spirit of fun and frolic that at times ran rampant there. To-day, while Brother Houston was visiting his brother in Chicago, who is connected with a publishing house, he procured a number of large cards with "Hogan's Alley" printed upon them, and hung them up through the car. There were also two swinging from the rear platform when the train left Chicago, much to the amusement of the people who were gathered at the station to see us off.

We reach Ft. Wayne at 9.30 P. M., and after a delay of a few minutes changing engines, start on our way again with P. Ft. W. & C. engine 272, Engineer M. Shea, Fireman E. Blanchard, Conductor T. J. Kanaga, Brakemen W. B. Kelley and A. C. Kyle, who take us to Crestline, Ohio, 132 miles. At the little station of Dixon, 20 miles east of Ft. Wayne, we cross the State line and enter Ohio. We are drawing nearer home and all feel very glad, although it will be like the breaking up of a large and happy family for us to separate. We expect to reach Pittsburgh early in the morning, and Brothers Haas and Schuler are saying goodbye, for Haas leaves us at Allegheny City and Schuler at Pittsburgh. It is approaching midnight, and as we skim across the State of Ohio we retire to our little beds and are soon fast asleep, lulled into repose by the soothing hum and motion of the train, that we have learned to regard as a great help to pleasant dreams and unbroken slumber.

## TUESDAY, JUNE 8th.

Getting up this morning about 5.30, I find we are approaching Allegheny City. It is a wet, foggy morning, and the Ohio River, in sight of which we are running, is high and muddy. We had changed engines at Crestline during the night, and now have P. Ft. W. & C. engine No. 288, Engineer Geo. Hood, Fireman F. Eberly, Conductor E. W. Davis, Brakemen E. W. Simpson and J. W. Syms, who take us into Pittsburgh, a run of 188 miles. When we stop in Allegheny City at six o'clock quite a number are astir to bid Brother Haas adieu; five minutes later we stop in Pittsburgh and part with Brother Schuler. Brother Sloane also leaves us here, as he has business to transact in the "Smoky City" before coming East.

Time changes here from Central to Eastern, one hour later, and we leave Pittsburgh at 7.17 A. M. with P. R. R. engine 1631, with Engineer M. Daily and Fireman S. K. Dobson in the cab. Our conductor is N. E. Garber and Brakemen W. J. Maxwell and Frank Dick. This crew runs us to Altoona, a distance of 117 miles, where we arrive at 10.35. After a delay of five minutes in changing engines we start on our way again with P. R. R. engine 646, in charge of Engineer H. Funk and Fireman E. Wilson. J. R. Bockus is conducting the train, whose brakemen are G. H. Free and G. W. Miller. Our train stops at Tyrone, 15 miles east of Altoona, to allow Brother and Mrs. Matthews to get off. They are obliged to leave us at this point, for they had left their little four-year-old daughter here in the care of relatives until their return and are longing to clasp Baby Ellie once more in their arms. This is a busy day with the members of the party and an interesting one for the porters. In a neat and characteristic speech Brother Reagan, in behalf of the lady occupants of the "Marco," presents Dennis Jackson with a substantial token of their appreciation of his kindness and courtesy toward them during the trip, they always finding him ready and willing to obey and oblige; and Dennis deserves their generous remembrance. Brother Sheppard, in behalf of the occupants of the "Milton," holds up Dick Pettus in the same manner and for the same purpose, and presents him with a generous token of their regard. Physically Dick is a giant, and all who know him will testify that he is as good-natured and kind as he is big and strong. The residents of "Hogan's Alley" ("Orchis") surround George Custis, while Brother Denniston in an eloquent speech tells him how good he is and how his goodness has been appreciated by the restive but good-natured and harmless inhabitants of this noted quarter, who desire to show their regard for the service he has rendered them by giving him a token of remembrance. George is worthy of their generosity, and quietly accepts the donation, saying to me as I pass him, "I often thought of the warning you gave me the day we started out."

Arriving in Harrisburg at 1.37 P. M. we bid adieu to Brothers Gilliland, Haefner, Smith, and their wives, also Brother McCarty, who leave us at this point, and changing engines for the last time we proceed on our way again with P. R. R. engine 296, Engineer H. B. Humphreys, Fireman J. Mahan, Conductor Dan. Harvey, Brakeman George Wilson. We are met in Harrisburg by a delegation from Philadelphia, composed of the following-named gentlemen, who constitute a Welcome Home Committee: Brothers John Mooney, Budd Roulon, George Stultz, Tony Hughes, Frank Vandyke, of West Philadelphia Division 162; J. Kelly and J. P. Anchor, of Camden Division 170; Trainmaster J. Thompson, Operator C. Devinney, and Baggagemaster Ed. Lynch, who accompany us to Philadelphia. They present each one of our party with a very pretty little white badge bearing the initials "O. R. C." in monogram and the inscription "Welcome Home" in golden letters. We have a number of badges and innumerable souvenirs that have been gathered on the trip, but not one among them all will be more highly prized than the little "Welcome Home" badge that bears silent but eloquent testimony to the deep fraternal sentiment that rejoices in our safe arrival home.

We have had a most wonderful trip; have traveled almost 9000 miles; no one has been injured and no one seriously sick. A prairie dog and a jack rabbit, so far as we can learn, are the only victims that met death by our train. We have crossed eighteen States and Territories, encountered no train robbers, experienced no wrecks, not having on a car during all our journey so much as a hot box or flat wheel.

Brother Layfield has been diligently obtaining punch cuts of the conductors he has met *en route*, and succeeded in obtaining forty-eight. Had they all been equipped with their punch that he met he would have had many more. The Colonel has been collecting punch marks for several years, and now has three hundred and fifty, nicely arranged in an album designed for the purpose. We are pained to learn that Brother Charles Larue, of

Camden Division 170, was thrown off his train yesterday and badly injured. He is a member of the Welcome Home Committee and had intended to accompany the rest to Harrisburg to meet us.

Our train rolls into Broad Street Station, Philadelphia, at 4.20 P. M., and we are warmly greeted by many friends who have gathered in the great train shed to welcome us home. From the station we are escorted to Odd Fellows' Temple, Broad and Cherry Streets, by the Reception Committee, representing West Philadelphia Division 162, Quaker City Division 204, Camden Division 170, and Wilmington Division 224. Brother J. H. Mooney, of Division 162, calls the meeting to order and in a neat little speech welcomes the excursionists home. Fine music is rendered by the Philharmonic Quintet, composed of the following gentlemen: Ed. Volmer, J. R. Whitely, Sol. Eicksteine, Chas. Genso, and Robert Crawford, ably led by Prof. Jo. Allen. Brothers Wyman, Sheppard, and Shaw are called upon for remarks relative to the trip, and they respond with short addresses. Songs and recitations are given by J. Conlin and Mr. and Mrs. Hughes, and the guests then repair to the basement banquet hall, where refreshments are served. At 7.30 the meeting adjourns, adieus are spoken, and we go to our several homes, feeling that we have had an extraordinary picnic in the thirty-two days of our outing, and hoping to meet again at the first anniversary of the Golden Gate Club one year hence.

[THE END.]

www.ingramcontent.com/pod-product-compliance
Lightning Source LLC
Chambersburg PA
CBHW021201230426
43667CB00006B/495